50 Japanese Cooking Guide Recipes for Home

By: Kelly Johnson

Table of Contents

- Sushi rolls
- Miso soup
- Teriyaki chicken
- Tempura vegetables
- Ramen noodles
- Yakitori skewers
- Gyoza dumplings
- Chirashi sushi
- Okonomiyaki pancakes
- Udon noodle soup
- Tonkatsu pork cutlets
- Donburi rice bowls
- Sashimi platter
- Takoyaki octopus balls
- Matcha green tea desserts
- Onigiri rice balls
- Japanese curry
- Shabu-shabu hot pot
- Oyakodon chicken and egg rice bowl
- Agedashi tofu
- Katsu-don pork cutlet rice bowl
- Nikujaga beef and potato stew
- Tamago egg sushi
- Chawanmushi savory egg custard
- Sunomono cucumber salad
- Anmitsu fruit jelly dessert
- Yaki soba fried noodles
- Hiyayakko cold tofu
- Zaru soba cold buckwheat noodles
- Dango sweet dumplings
- Mochi rice cakes
- Omurice omelette rice
- Nabemono hot pot dishes
- Taiyaki fish-shaped cakes
- Dorayaki red bean pancakes

- Somen noodles with dipping sauce
- Yudofu hot tofu
- Mitarashi dango grilled skewered dumplings
- Hōtō miso soup with flat noodles
- Chikuwa fish cakes
- Kombu dashi broth
- Saba mackerel sushi
- Kaisendon seafood rice bowl
- Ankake yakisoba noodles with thick sauce
- Kinpira gobo sautéed burdock root
- Natto fermented soybeans
- Horenso no gomaae spinach salad with sesame dressing
- Saba shioyaki grilled salted mackerel
- Kurimu korokke creamy croquettes
- Matcha latte

Sushi rolls

Ingredients:

- Sushi rice (cooked and seasoned with rice vinegar, sugar, and salt)
- Nori (seaweed) sheets
- Fillings of your choice (such as cucumber, avocado, carrot, cooked shrimp, smoked salmon, crab sticks, etc.)
- Soy sauce, wasabi, and pickled ginger (for serving)

Instructions:

1. Prepare the Rice:
    - Cook sushi rice according to the package instructions.
    - Once cooked, season the rice with rice vinegar, sugar, and salt. Allow it to cool to room temperature.
2. Prepare the Fillings:
    - Prepare your desired fillings by slicing them into thin strips or pieces. Common fillings include cucumber, avocado, carrot, and seafood.
3. Assemble the Rolls:
    - Place a nori sheet on a clean bamboo sushi mat (makisu), shiny side down.
    - With wet hands, spread a thin layer of sushi rice evenly over the nori sheet, leaving about 1 inch of the nori sheet uncovered at the top.
    - Arrange your desired fillings horizontally across the center of the rice.
4. Roll the Sushi:
    - Lift the bottom edge of the bamboo mat with both hands and roll it over the fillings, using your fingers to tuck the fillings in tightly.
    - Continue rolling until the entire nori sheet is wrapped around the fillings.
    - Apply gentle pressure to the roll with the bamboo mat to shape it into a tight cylinder.
5. Slice the Rolls:
    - Use a sharp knife to slice the sushi roll into individual pieces, about 1 inch thick. Wet the knife with water between cuts to prevent sticking.
6. Serve:
    - Arrange the sushi rolls on a plate and serve with soy sauce, wasabi, and pickled ginger on the side.

7. Enjoy!
    - Enjoy your homemade sushi rolls as a delicious appetizer or main course.

Feel free to customize your sushi rolls with different fillings and toppings according to your taste preferences!

Miso soup

Ingredients:

- 4 cups water
- 4 tablespoons miso paste (white or red, depending on preference)
- 2 green onions, thinly sliced
- 1 block (about 200g) silken tofu, cubed
- 1 sheet nori (seaweed), cut into thin strips (optional)
- 1 tablespoon soy sauce (optional)
- Optional additions: sliced mushrooms, wakame seaweed, cooked shrimp, tofu skins, etc.

Instructions:

1. Prepare the Broth:
   - In a pot, bring the water to a gentle boil over medium heat.
2. Add Miso Paste:
   - Once the water is simmering, reduce the heat to low. Take a ladleful of hot water and place it in a small bowl. Add the miso paste to the bowl and whisk until smooth.
3. Combine Miso Paste with Broth:
   - Pour the miso mixture back into the pot of simmering water, stirring gently to combine. Be careful not to let the soup come to a boil once the miso has been added, as boiling can reduce its flavor.
4. Add Tofu and Green Onions:
   - Add the cubed tofu and sliced green onions to the pot. Let the soup simmer for a few minutes until the tofu is heated through and the green onions are softened.
5. Optional Additions:
   - If using, add any optional ingredients such as sliced mushrooms, wakame seaweed, cooked shrimp, tofu skins, etc., and simmer until they are cooked through.
6. Season to Taste:
   - Taste the soup and adjust the seasoning if necessary. You can add a tablespoon of soy sauce for extra flavor if desired.
7. Serve:
   - Ladle the miso soup into bowls and garnish with nori strips if using. Serve hot and enjoy as a comforting and nourishing meal or starter.

Miso soup is versatile, so feel free to customize it with your favorite ingredients to suit your taste preferences.

Teriyaki chicken

Ingredients:

- 4 boneless, skinless chicken breasts
- 1/2 cup soy sauce (or tamari for gluten-free)
- 1/4 cup mirin (Japanese sweet rice wine)
- 1/4 cup sake (Japanese rice wine) or dry sherry
- 2 tablespoons brown sugar or honey
- 2 cloves garlic, minced
- 1 teaspoon grated ginger
- 1 tablespoon vegetable oil
- Sesame seeds and sliced green onions for garnish (optional)

Instructions:

1. Prepare the Chicken:
    - Pat the chicken breasts dry with paper towels. Slice them horizontally into thinner pieces for faster and more even cooking.
2. Make the Teriyaki Sauce:
    - In a bowl, whisk together the soy sauce, mirin, sake, brown sugar (or honey), minced garlic, and grated ginger until well combined. This will be your teriyaki sauce.
3. Marinate the Chicken:
    - Place the chicken pieces in a shallow dish or a resealable plastic bag. Pour about half of the teriyaki sauce over the chicken, reserving the other half for later. Make sure the chicken is evenly coated. Marinate in the refrigerator for at least 30 minutes, or up to 4 hours for maximum flavor.
4. Cook the Chicken:
    - Heat the vegetable oil in a large skillet or grill pan over medium-high heat. Once hot, add the chicken pieces in a single layer, making sure not to overcrowd the pan. Cook for about 5-6 minutes on each side, or until the chicken is cooked through and nicely caramelized, basting occasionally with the remaining teriyaki sauce.
5. Garnish and Serve:
    - Once the chicken is cooked, remove it from the pan and transfer it to a serving plate. Sprinkle with sesame seeds and sliced green onions for

garnish if desired. Serve hot with rice and steamed vegetables, drizzling any remaining teriyaki sauce over the chicken.

6. Enjoy!
   - Serve your delicious homemade teriyaki chicken and enjoy the savory-sweet flavors of this classic Japanese dish.

Feel free to adjust the sweetness or saltiness of the teriyaki sauce to suit your taste preferences. You can also add a splash of water if the sauce becomes too thick during cooking.

Tempura vegetables

Ingredients:

For the Tempura Batter:

- 1 cup all-purpose flour
- 1/2 cup cornstarch
- 1 teaspoon baking powder
- 1 cup ice-cold water
- Pinch of salt
- Ice cubes

For the Vegetables:

- Assorted vegetables such as:
    - Broccoli florets
    - Sliced bell peppers
    - Sliced carrots
    - Zucchini rounds
    - Green beans
    - Sweet potato slices
- Vegetable oil for frying

For Dipping Sauce:

- 1/4 cup soy sauce
- 2 tablespoons rice vinegar
- 1 tablespoon mirin (Japanese sweet rice wine)
- 1 teaspoon grated ginger
- 1 teaspoon grated daikon radish (optional)
- 1 teaspoon chopped green onion (optional)

Instructions:

1. Prepare the Vegetables:
   - Wash and dry the vegetables thoroughly. Cut them into bite-sized pieces or strips, ensuring they are all relatively uniform in size for even cooking.
2. Prepare the Dipping Sauce:
   - In a small bowl, mix together the soy sauce, rice vinegar, mirin, grated ginger, grated daikon radish (if using), and chopped green onion (if using). Set aside.
3. Make the Tempura Batter:
   - In a large mixing bowl, combine the all-purpose flour, cornstarch, baking powder, and a pinch of salt. Gradually add the ice-cold water while stirring gently. Be careful not to overmix; lumps are okay. The batter should be thin and slightly lumpy.
   - Add a handful of ice cubes to the batter to keep it cold. This helps create a crispier tempura coating.
4. Heat the Oil:
   - In a deep fryer or large pot, heat vegetable oil to 350°F (180°C). The oil should be hot enough to quickly cook the vegetables and create a crispy coating without absorbing too much oil.
5. Coat the Vegetables:
   - Dip the prepared vegetables into the tempura batter, ensuring they are fully coated. Shake off any excess batter.
6. Fry the Tempura:
   - Carefully place the battered vegetables into the hot oil, a few pieces at a time, making sure not to overcrowd the pot. Fry in batches if necessary.
   - Fry the vegetables for 2-3 minutes, or until they are golden brown and crispy. Use a slotted spoon or tongs to remove them from the oil and transfer them to a plate lined with paper towels to drain excess oil.
7. Serve:
   - Serve the tempura vegetables immediately while they are still hot and crispy. Enjoy them with the dipping sauce on the side.
8. Enjoy!
   - Serve your crispy tempura vegetables as a delicious appetizer or side dish, and enjoy the crunchy texture and savory flavor.

Ramen noodles

Ingredients:

For the Noodles:

- 2 cups all-purpose flour
- 1/2 teaspoon salt
- 2 large eggs

For the Soup Base (optional):

- 4 cups chicken or vegetable broth
- 2 cloves garlic, minced
- 1 tablespoon grated ginger
- 2 tablespoons soy sauce
- 1 tablespoon mirin (Japanese sweet rice wine) or rice vinegar
- 1 teaspoon sesame oil
- Salt and pepper to taste

For Toppings (optional):

- Sliced cooked chicken, pork, or tofu
- Soft-boiled eggs
- Sliced green onions
- Sliced mushrooms
- Bean sprouts
- Nori (seaweed)
- Bamboo shoots
- Corn kernels
- Chili oil or Sriracha (for extra heat)

Instructions:

1. Prepare the Noodle Dough:
   - In a large mixing bowl, combine the all-purpose flour and salt. Make a well in the center and add the eggs.
   - Using a fork or your fingers, gradually incorporate the flour into the eggs until a rough dough forms.
   - Turn the dough out onto a clean, floured surface and knead for about 5-10 minutes, or until the dough becomes smooth and elastic.
   - Wrap the dough in plastic wrap and let it rest at room temperature for at least 30 minutes to allow the gluten to relax.
2. Roll and Cut the Noodles:
   - After resting, divide the dough into 4 equal portions. Working with one portion at a time, flatten it into a rectangular shape with a rolling pin.
   - Dust the dough lightly with flour and roll it out into a thin sheet, about 1/16 inch thick.
   - Fold the sheet of dough in half lengthwise and then in half again. Use a sharp knife to cut the folded dough into thin strips to form noodles.
   - Unfold the noodles and gently toss them with flour to prevent sticking. Repeat with the remaining portions of dough.
3. Cook the Noodles:
   - Bring a large pot of water to a boil. Add the fresh ramen noodles and cook for 2-3 minutes, or until they are tender but still chewy (al dente). Be careful not to overcook.
   - Once cooked, drain the noodles and rinse them under cold water to stop the cooking process. Set aside.
4. Prepare the Soup Base (optional):
   - In a separate pot, combine the chicken or vegetable broth with minced garlic, grated ginger, soy sauce, mirin or rice vinegar, and sesame oil. Bring to a simmer and cook for a few minutes to allow the flavors to meld together. Season with salt and pepper to taste.
5. Assemble the Ramen Bowls:
   - Divide the cooked noodles among serving bowls. Ladle the hot soup base over the noodles.
   - Add your desired toppings, such as sliced cooked chicken, pork, or tofu, soft-boiled eggs, sliced green onions, sliced mushrooms, bean sprouts, nori, bamboo shoots, corn kernels, and a drizzle of chili oil or Sriracha for extra heat.
6. Serve and Enjoy!

- Serve your homemade ramen noodles hot and enjoy the comforting and flavorful bowl of soup. Adjust the seasoning and toppings according to your taste preferences.

Yakitori skewers

Ingredients:

For the Yakitori Sauce:

- 1/2 cup soy sauce
- 1/4 cup mirin (Japanese sweet rice wine)
- 1/4 cup sake (Japanese rice wine) or dry sherry
- 2 tablespoons brown sugar or honey
- 2 cloves garlic, minced
- 1 teaspoon grated ginger
- 1 tablespoon cornstarch (optional, for thickening)

For the Skewers:

- 1 lb (450g) boneless, skinless chicken thighs or chicken breast, cut into bite-sized pieces
- Bamboo skewers, soaked in water for at least 30 minutes to prevent burning
- Optional: Sliced green onions for garnish

Instructions:

1. Prepare the Yakitori Sauce:
    - In a saucepan, combine the soy sauce, mirin, sake, brown sugar (or honey), minced garlic, and grated ginger. Bring to a simmer over medium heat, stirring occasionally to dissolve the sugar.
    - If you prefer a thicker sauce, mix the cornstarch with a tablespoon of water to make a slurry. Stir the slurry into the sauce and cook for an additional 1-2 minutes until the sauce thickens slightly. Remove from heat and let the sauce cool.
2. Prepare the Skewers:
    - Thread the chicken pieces onto the soaked bamboo skewers, leaving a little space between each piece to ensure even cooking.
3. Grill the Skewers:
    - Preheat your grill to medium-high heat. If using a charcoal grill, wait until the coals are hot and glowing.

- Place the skewers on the grill and cook for 3-4 minutes on each side, or until the chicken is cooked through and nicely caramelized. Baste the skewers with the yakitori sauce occasionally during cooking to add flavor and moisture.
- Make sure to turn the skewers frequently to prevent burning and to cook the chicken evenly.

4. Serve:
    - Once the chicken is cooked, remove the skewers from the grill and place them on a serving platter.
    - Brush the cooked chicken skewers with extra yakitori sauce and sprinkle with sliced green onions for garnish if desired.

5. Enjoy!
    - Serve the yakitori skewers hot as an appetizer or main dish. They're perfect for sharing with friends and family, and the sweet-savory flavor of the yakitori sauce is sure to be a hit!

Gyoza dumplings

Ingredients:

For the Gyoza Filling:

- 1/2 lb (about 225g) ground pork (you can also use ground chicken or turkey)
- 1 cup cabbage, finely chopped
- 2 green onions, finely chopped
- 2 cloves garlic, minced
- 1 teaspoon ginger, grated
- 1 tablespoon soy sauce
- 1 tablespoon sesame oil
- 1 teaspoon sugar
- Salt and pepper to taste

For the Gyoza Wrappers:

- 30 round gyoza wrappers (you can find these at Asian grocery stores or make your own)

For Dipping Sauce:

- 1/4 cup soy sauce
- 2 tablespoons rice vinegar
- 1 teaspoon sesame oil
- 1 teaspoon sugar
- Red pepper flakes or chili oil (optional, for extra heat)

Instructions:

1. Prepare the Gyoza Filling:
    - In a large mixing bowl, combine the ground pork, chopped cabbage, chopped green onions, minced garlic, grated ginger, soy sauce, sesame oil, sugar, salt, and pepper. Mix well until all ingredients are evenly incorporated.
2. Assemble the Gyoza Dumplings:

- Place a small amount of filling (about 1 tablespoon) in the center of each gyoza wrapper.
- Moisten the edges of the wrapper with water using your fingertip.
- Fold the wrapper in half over the filling to create a half-moon shape. Pinch the edges together to seal, pleating one side of the wrapper as you go, if desired. Press firmly to ensure the seal is tight.

3. Cook the Gyoza:
    - Heat a large non-stick skillet over medium-high heat. Add a small amount of vegetable oil to coat the bottom of the skillet.
    - Place the gyoza dumplings in a single layer in the skillet, flat side down. Cook for 2-3 minutes, or until the bottoms are golden brown.
    - Carefully add about 1/4 cup of water to the skillet and immediately cover with a lid to create steam. Cook for an additional 4-5 minutes, or until the filling is cooked through and the wrappers are translucent.
4. Make the Dipping Sauce:
    - While the gyoza are cooking, prepare the dipping sauce by combining soy sauce, rice vinegar, sesame oil, and sugar in a small bowl. Add red pepper flakes or chili oil for extra heat if desired. Stir well to combine.
5. Serve:
    - Once the gyoza dumplings are cooked, remove them from the skillet and transfer to a serving plate.
    - Serve the gyoza hot with the dipping sauce on the side.
6. Enjoy!
    - Enjoy your homemade gyoza dumplings as a delicious appetizer or main dish. They're perfect for sharing with friends and family, and the combination of savory filling and dipping sauce is sure to be a hit!

Chirashi sushi

Ingredients:

For the Sushi Rice:

- 2 cups sushi rice
- 2 cups water
- 1/4 cup rice vinegar
- 2 tablespoons sugar
- 1 teaspoon salt

For the Toppings (suggestions, feel free to customize):

- Sashimi-grade fish (such as tuna, salmon, yellowtail, or shrimp), thinly sliced
- Cooked shrimp, peeled and deveined
- Tamagoyaki (Japanese rolled omelette), thinly sliced
- Cucumber, thinly sliced
- Avocado, sliced
- Radish sprouts (kaiware)
- Pickled ginger (gari)
- Wasabi paste
- Sesame seeds
- Nori (seaweed), cut into thin strips
- Shiso leaves, thinly sliced

Instructions:

1. Prepare the Sushi Rice:
    - Rinse the sushi rice in a fine-mesh sieve under cold water until the water runs clear.
    - In a rice cooker or a medium saucepan, combine the rinsed rice and water. Cook according to the rice cooker instructions or bring to a boil, then reduce the heat to low, cover, and simmer for 15-20 minutes until the rice is cooked and the water is absorbed.

- In a small saucepan, combine the rice vinegar, sugar, and salt. Heat over low heat, stirring occasionally, until the sugar and salt are dissolved. Remove from heat.
- Transfer the cooked rice to a large mixing bowl and gently fold in the seasoned rice vinegar until well combined. Let the rice cool to room temperature.

2. Prepare the Toppings:
   - Prepare the sashimi-grade fish by slicing it thinly. You can also prepare cooked shrimp, tamagoyaki, cucumber, avocado, radish sprouts, pickled ginger, wasabi paste, sesame seeds, nori, and shiso leaves.
3. Assemble the Chirashi Sushi:
   - Divide the sushi rice among serving bowls.
   - Arrange the prepared toppings on top of the rice in an attractive and colorful pattern. Be creative with the arrangement, scattering the toppings evenly over the rice.
   - Garnish with additional sesame seeds, nori strips, and shiso leaves for extra flavor and visual appeal.
4. Serve:
   - Serve the chirashi sushi bowls with soy sauce, pickled ginger, and wasabi paste on the side.
5. Enjoy!
   - Enjoy your homemade chirashi sushi as a beautiful and delicious meal. It's perfect for special occasions or anytime you're craving a fresh and satisfying dish!

Okonomiyaki pancakes

Ingredients:

For the Batter:

- 2 cups all-purpose flour
- 1 1/2 cups dashi stock or water
- 2 large eggs
- 1/2 teaspoon salt
- 1/4 teaspoon baking powder

For the Filling (Choose from the following or mix and match):

- Thinly sliced cabbage
- Thinly sliced pork belly, cooked shrimp, or diced cooked chicken
- Sliced green onions
- Grated carrots
- Chopped mushrooms
- Tempura scraps (tenkasu)
- Sliced squid or octopus
- Thinly sliced kamaboko (fish cake)
- Bean sprouts

For Toppings:

- Okonomiyaki sauce (or a mixture of Worcestershire sauce and ketchup)
- Japanese mayonnaise
- Aonori (dried seaweed flakes)
- Katsuobushi (dried bonito flakes)
- Pickled ginger (beni shoga)

Instructions:

1. Prepare the Batter:

- In a large mixing bowl, whisk together the all-purpose flour, dashi stock (or water), eggs, salt, and baking powder until smooth. The batter should be thick but pourable.
2. Prepare the Filling:
    - Prepare your desired filling ingredients by slicing or chopping them into small pieces.
3. Mix the Batter and Filling:
    - Add the prepared filling ingredients to the batter and mix until well combined. The batter should be evenly distributed throughout the filling ingredients.
4. Cook the Pancakes:
    - Heat a large non-stick skillet or griddle over medium heat. Add a small amount of vegetable oil to the pan.
    - Pour a portion of the batter onto the hot skillet to form a pancake, about 6-8 inches in diameter. Use a spatula to spread the batter evenly and flatten it slightly.
    - Cook the pancake for 4-5 minutes on one side, or until golden brown and crispy. Flip the pancake and cook for an additional 4-5 minutes on the other side until cooked through and crispy.
5. Serve:
    - Transfer the cooked okonomiyaki pancake to a serving plate.
    - Drizzle okonomiyaki sauce and Japanese mayonnaise over the pancake in a zigzag pattern.
    - Sprinkle with aonori and katsuobushi.
    - Garnish with pickled ginger on the side.
6. Enjoy!
    - Cut the okonomiyaki pancake into wedges and enjoy it hot as a delicious and satisfying meal. It's perfect for sharing with friends and family, and you can customize it with your favorite fillings and toppings!

Udon noodle soup

Ingredients:

For the Soup Base:

- 6 cups dashi stock (or vegetable broth for a vegetarian version)
- 1/4 cup soy sauce
- 2 tablespoons mirin (Japanese sweet rice wine)
- 1 tablespoon sake (Japanese rice wine) or dry sherry
- 2 teaspoons sugar
- 1 teaspoon salt

For the Toppings (choose from the following or mix and match):

- Cooked chicken, beef, pork, or shrimp
- Firm tofu, sliced
- Sliced green onions
- Shiitake mushrooms, sliced
- Baby spinach or bok choy leaves
- Kamaboko (fish cake), sliced
- Nori (seaweed), cut into thin strips
- Soft-boiled egg, halved

For the Udon Noodles:

- 8 ounces (about 225g) dried udon noodles or fresh udon noodles
- Water for boiling

Instructions:

1. Prepare the Soup Base:
    - In a large pot, combine the dashi stock, soy sauce, mirin, sake, sugar, and salt. Bring to a simmer over medium heat, stirring occasionally to dissolve the sugar and salt. Reduce the heat to low and let the soup simmer gently while you prepare the toppings and noodles.
2. Prepare the Toppings:

- Cook any raw protein such as chicken, beef, pork, or shrimp if using. Slice into bite-sized pieces.
- If using tofu, slice it into cubes and lightly pan-fry until golden brown.
- Slice green onions, shiitake mushrooms, kamaboko, and any other toppings you've chosen.

3. Cook the Udon Noodles:
    - If using dried udon noodles, cook them according to the package instructions in a separate pot of boiling water until they are tender but still chewy, usually about 8-10 minutes. If using fresh udon noodles, they may only need 1-2 minutes to cook.
    - Drain the cooked noodles and rinse them under cold water to stop the cooking process. Set aside.
4. Assemble the Udon Noodle Soup:
    - Divide the cooked udon noodles among serving bowls.
    - Arrange the cooked toppings on top of the noodles in an attractive and colorful manner.
    - Ladle the hot soup base over the noodles and toppings, ensuring they are completely submerged in the broth.
5. Serve:
    - Garnish the udon noodle soup with sliced green onions, nori strips, and soft-boiled egg halves if desired.
    - Serve the udon noodle soup hot and enjoy it as a comforting and satisfying meal.
6. Enjoy!
    - Enjoy your homemade udon noodle soup as a delicious and nourishing dish. Feel free to customize it with your favorite toppings and adjust the seasoning according to your taste preferences!

Tonkatsu pork cutlets

Ingredients:

For the Tonkatsu:

- 4 boneless pork loin chops, about 1/2 inch thick
- Salt and pepper to taste
- All-purpose flour for dredging
- 2 large eggs, beaten
- Panko breadcrumbs (Japanese breadcrumbs)
- Vegetable oil for frying

For Serving:

- Tonkatsu sauce (store-bought or homemade)
- Shredded cabbage
- Cooked rice

Instructions:

1. Prepare the Pork Cutlets:
    - Use a meat mallet to pound the pork chops to an even thickness, about 1/4 inch thick. Season both sides of the pork chops with salt and pepper.
2. Set Up a Breading Station:
    - Set up a breading station with three shallow bowls. Place the all-purpose flour in the first bowl, beaten eggs in the second bowl, and panko breadcrumbs in the third bowl.
3. Bread the Pork Cutlets:
    - Dredge each pork chop in the flour, shaking off any excess.
    - Dip the floured pork chops into the beaten eggs, allowing any excess egg to drip off.
    - Coat the pork chops with panko breadcrumbs, pressing gently to adhere the breadcrumbs to the surface of the meat. Make sure the pork chops are evenly coated with breadcrumbs.
4. Fry the Tonkatsu:
    - Heat vegetable oil in a large skillet or deep fryer to 350°F (180°C).

- Carefully place the breaded pork chops into the hot oil, working in batches if necessary to avoid overcrowding the pan.
- Fry the pork chops for 3-4 minutes on each side, or until they are golden brown and cooked through. The internal temperature of the pork should reach 145°F (63°C).
- Remove the tonkatsu from the oil and drain them on a wire rack or paper towels to remove excess oil.

5. Serve:
   - Slice the tonkatsu into strips or bite-sized pieces.
   - Serve the tonkatsu hot with shredded cabbage and tonkatsu sauce on the side. You can also serve it with cooked rice for a complete meal.

6. Enjoy!
   - Enjoy your homemade tonkatsu pork cutlets as a delicious and satisfying meal. The crispy exterior and tender pork inside, paired with the tangy tonkatsu sauce and crunchy cabbage, make for a truly irresistible dish!

Donburi rice bowls

Ingredients:

For the Donburi Base:

- Cooked Japanese short-grain rice

For the Toppings (Choose from the following or mix and match):

- Chicken Teriyaki: Grilled or pan-fried chicken thighs glazed with teriyaki sauce
- Beef Gyudon: Thinly sliced beef simmered in a sweet and savory broth with onions
- Pork Katsudon: Breaded and deep-fried pork cutlets topped with eggs and simmered in a soy-based sauce
- Tofu Donburi: Crispy fried tofu cubes seasoned with soy sauce and mirin
- Ebi (Shrimp) Tempura Donburi: Crispy fried shrimp tempura
- Unagi (Grilled Eel) Donburi: Grilled eel glazed with sweet soy sauce
- Tamago (Egg) Donburi: Sweet rolled omelette sliced and served over rice

For Garnish (optional):

- Sliced green onions
- Toasted sesame seeds
- Nori (seaweed) flakes
- Pickled ginger (beni shoga)

For Sauce (optional):

- Teriyaki sauce
- Soy sauce
- Mirin (Japanese sweet rice wine)
- Dashi stock
- Oyster sauce

Instructions:

1. Prepare the Donburi Toppings:
   - Cook your chosen protein (chicken, beef, pork, tofu, shrimp, or eel) according to the specific recipe instructions. Make sure it's cooked through and seasoned to your liking.
2. Cook the Rice:
   - Rinse Japanese short-grain rice until the water runs clear. Cook the rice according to the package instructions or using a rice cooker until fluffy and tender.
3. Assemble the Donburi Bowls:
   - Divide the cooked rice among serving bowls to form the base of the donburi.
   - Arrange the cooked toppings over the rice in an attractive manner. If using eggs (as in katsudon or tamago donburi), beat them and pour them over the hot toppings to cook slightly from the residual heat.
4. Drizzle with Sauce (optional):
   - Drizzle the donburi toppings with your choice of sauce, such as teriyaki sauce, soy sauce, mirin, dashi stock, or oyster sauce, depending on the recipe you're following.
5. Garnish (optional):
   - Sprinkle the donburi bowls with sliced green onions, toasted sesame seeds, nori flakes, or pickled ginger for extra flavor and texture.
6. Serve:
   - Serve the donburi bowls immediately while hot.
7. Enjoy!
   - Enjoy your homemade donburi rice bowls as a delicious and satisfying meal. Each bite combines the savory flavors of the toppings with the fluffy texture of the rice for a truly comforting dining experience.

Sashimi platter

Ingredients:

For the Sashimi:

- Assorted sashimi-grade fish (such as tuna, salmon, yellowtail, snapper, mackerel, or squid)
- Optional: Shellfish (such as scallops, shrimp, or octopus)
- Optional: Tamagoyaki (Japanese rolled omelette)

For Garnish:

- Shiso leaves (perilla leaves)
- Radish sprouts (kaiware)
- Edible flowers
- Lemon or lime wedges
- Daikon radish, thinly sliced
- Pickled ginger (gari)

For Dipping Sauce:

- Soy sauce
- Wasabi paste
- Pickled ginger (gari)

Instructions:

1. Prepare the Fish:
    - Start by selecting the freshest sashimi-grade fish available. Ensure that it has been properly cleaned and prepared for raw consumption. Slice the fish into thin slices, cutting against the grain for optimal texture.
2. Arrange the Sashimi:
    - Choose a large platter or wooden board as the base for your sashimi presentation.

- Arrange the sliced sashimi on the platter in an attractive and visually appealing manner. You can arrange the slices in rows or fan them out in a circular pattern. Leave some space between each slice for garnishes.
3. Add Garnishes:
    - Garnish the sashimi platter with shiso leaves, radish sprouts, edible flowers, lemon or lime wedges, and thinly sliced daikon radish. These garnishes not only add color and texture but also complement the flavors of the sashimi.
4. Optional Additions:
    - If desired, include additional elements on the platter such as tamagoyaki (Japanese rolled omelette) slices or shellfish like scallops, shrimp, or octopus. These can add variety and interest to the platter.
5. Serve with Dipping Sauce:
    - Serve the sashimi platter with a small bowl of soy sauce for dipping, along with wasabi paste and pickled ginger on the side. Encourage guests to mix the wasabi into the soy sauce to create their own dipping sauce.
6. Presentation:
    - Present the sashimi platter as the centerpiece of your meal or as part of a larger spread. It's best served immediately to ensure the freshness of the fish.
7. Enjoy!
    - Enjoy your homemade sashimi platter as a delightful and elegant dish that highlights the delicate flavors of the fish. It's perfect for special occasions or as a luxurious treat for yourself and your guests.

Takoyaki octopus balls

Ingredients:

For the Takoyaki Batter:

- 2 cups takoyaki flour (or all-purpose flour)
- 4 large eggs
- 3 1/2 cups dashi stock (or water)
- 1/2 teaspoon salt
- 1 tablespoon soy sauce
- 2 tablespoons cooking oil

For Filling and Toppings:

- 1 cup diced cooked octopus (or substitute with cooked shrimp, squid, or vegetables)
- Takoyaki sauce (store-bought or homemade)
- Japanese mayonnaise
- Aonori (dried seaweed flakes)
- Katsuobushi (bonito flakes)
- Pickled ginger (beni shoga)

Instructions:

1. Prepare the Takoyaki Batter:
    - In a large mixing bowl, combine the takoyaki flour, eggs, dashi stock (or water), salt, and soy sauce. Whisk until smooth and well combined.
2. Heat the Takoyaki Pan:
    - Preheat a takoyaki pan over medium heat. Brush each mold with a thin layer of cooking oil to prevent sticking.
3. Fill the Takoyaki Molds:
    - Once the pan is hot, pour the batter into each mold, filling them nearly to the top. Add a piece of diced octopus (or your preferred filling) into each mold.
4. Cook the Takoyaki:

- Using a skewer or takoyaki pick, continuously rotate the batter around each mold to form a spherical shape. As the batter begins to set, continue rotating and shaping until the takoyaki becomes golden brown and crispy on the outside, about 5-7 minutes.

5. Flip the Takoyaki:
    - Carefully flip each takoyaki ball using the skewer or takoyaki pick, ensuring that the uncooked batter flows into the bottom of the mold. Continue cooking until the other side is golden brown and crispy, about 5-7 minutes.
6. Serve the Takoyaki:
    - Once the takoyaki balls are cooked through and crispy on all sides, transfer them to a serving plate.
7. Add Toppings:
    - Drizzle takoyaki sauce and Japanese mayonnaise over the top of the takoyaki balls. Sprinkle with aonori and katsuobushi for extra flavor. Garnish with pickled ginger.
8. Serve Hot:
    - Serve the takoyaki octopus balls immediately while hot and enjoy them as a delicious and satisfying snack or appetizer.
9. Enjoy!
    - Enjoy your homemade takoyaki octopus balls with friends and family, and savor the crispy exterior and tender octopus filling. They're perfect for sharing and are sure to be a hit at any gathering!

Matcha green tea desserts

Matcha Green Tea Cheesecake Bars:

Ingredients:

For the Crust:

- 1 1/2 cups graham cracker crumbs
- 1/4 cup granulated sugar
- 6 tablespoons unsalted butter, melted

For the Filling:

- 2 (8-ounce) packages cream cheese, softened
- 2/3 cup granulated sugar
- 2 large eggs
- 2 tablespoons matcha green tea powder
- 1 teaspoon vanilla extract
- 1/2 cup sour cream

For the Topping (Optional):

- Whipped cream
- Matcha powder for dusting

Instructions:

1. Preheat the Oven:
    - Preheat your oven to 325°F (160°C). Grease a 9x9-inch baking pan or line it with parchment paper, leaving an overhang for easy removal.
2. Make the Crust:
    - In a medium bowl, mix together the graham cracker crumbs, sugar, and melted butter until well combined. Press the mixture evenly into the bottom of the prepared baking pan.
3. Prepare the Filling:

- In a large mixing bowl, beat the softened cream cheese and granulated sugar with an electric mixer until smooth and creamy.
- Add the eggs, one at a time, mixing well after each addition.
- Stir in the matcha green tea powder and vanilla extract until fully incorporated.
- Fold in the sour cream until smooth and well combined.

4. Assemble and Bake:
   - Pour the cheesecake filling over the prepared crust in the baking pan, spreading it out evenly.
   - Tap the pan gently on the counter to remove any air bubbles.
   - Bake in the preheated oven for 35-40 minutes, or until the edges are set and the center is slightly jiggly.
   - Remove from the oven and let the cheesecake cool completely in the pan on a wire rack.

5. Chill and Serve:
   - Once cooled, refrigerate the cheesecake bars for at least 4 hours, or overnight, until fully chilled and set.
   - Once chilled, use the parchment overhang to lift the cheesecake out of the pan and onto a cutting board.
   - Cut into squares or bars using a sharp knife.
   - Optional: Top each bar with a dollop of whipped cream and dust with matcha powder before serving.

6. Enjoy!
   - Serve your Matcha Green Tea Cheesecake Bars chilled and enjoy the creamy texture and earthy matcha flavor with every bite. They make a delightful dessert or snack for any occasion!

Onigiri rice balls

Ingredients:

For the Rice:

- 2 cups Japanese short-grain rice (also known as sushi rice)
- 2 1/2 cups water
- Rice vinegar (optional)
- Salt (optional)

For Filling (Optional):

- Salted salmon
- Pickled plum (umeboshi)
- Grilled chicken
- Tuna salad
- Cooked shrimp
- Seasoned vegetables (such as cooked spinach or sautéed mushrooms)

For Seasoning and Garnish (Optional):

- Nori (seaweed) sheets, cut into thin strips
- Toasted sesame seeds
- Furikake (Japanese rice seasoning)
- Soy sauce
- Wasabi

Instructions:

1. Prepare the Rice:
   - Rinse the rice in cold water until the water runs clear to remove excess starch. Drain well.
   - Combine the rinsed rice and water in a rice cooker or pot. Cook the rice according to the manufacturer's instructions or until it's cooked and fluffy.
2. Season the Rice (Optional):

- While the rice is still hot, season it with a mixture of rice vinegar and salt. Use about 2 tablespoons of rice vinegar and 1 tablespoon of sugar for every 2 cups of cooked rice. Mix gently to combine.
3. Prepare the Filling (Optional):
    - If using fillings like salted salmon or grilled chicken, make sure they are cooked and seasoned to your liking. Shred or chop them into small pieces.
4. Shape the Onigiri:
    - Moisten your hands with water to prevent the rice from sticking. Scoop a small portion of cooked rice into one hand (about 1/3 to 1/2 cup).
    - Make an indentation in the center of the rice and place a small amount of filling (if using) in the indentation.
    - Close your hand to encase the filling and shape the rice into a triangle or ball. Press firmly to compact the rice.
    - If desired, wrap a strip of nori around the base of the onigiri to hold it together and add flavor.
5. Garnish the Onigiri (Optional):
    - Sprinkle the onigiri with toasted sesame seeds, furikake, or other seasonings of your choice.
6. Serve and Enjoy:
    - Serve the onigiri at room temperature or slightly warm. They are best enjoyed fresh but can also be packed for lunch or a snack on the go.
7. Variations:
    - Experiment with different fillings and seasonings to create your own unique onigiri flavors. You can also try shaping the onigiri into different shapes, such as hearts or cylinders, for a fun twist.
8. Enjoy!
    - Enjoy your homemade onigiri rice balls as a delicious and satisfying snack or light meal. They're perfect for picnics, lunchboxes, or anytime you're craving a taste of Japan!

Japanese curry

Ingredients:

- 2 tablespoons vegetable oil
- 1 onion, chopped
- 2 carrots, peeled and diced
- 2 potatoes, peeled and diced
- 1 pound (450g) protein of your choice (chicken, beef, pork, tofu, or a combination), cut into bite-sized pieces
- 3 cups water or chicken/beef broth
- 2-3 tablespoons Japanese curry roux (available in stores or homemade)
- Salt and pepper to taste
- Optional: additional vegetables such as bell peppers, peas, or mushrooms
- Cooked rice, for serving

Japanese Curry Roux Ingredients (if making from scratch):

- 3 tablespoons butter
- 4 tablespoons all-purpose flour
- 2 tablespoons curry powder
- 1 tablespoon garam masala (optional)
- 1 tablespoon tomato paste
- 1 tablespoon soy sauce
- 1 tablespoon Worcestershire sauce
- 1 teaspoon sugar
- 2 cups water or broth

Instructions:

1. Prepare the Curry Roux (if making from scratch):
   - In a saucepan, melt the butter over medium heat. Add the flour and curry powder, and cook, stirring constantly, for 2-3 minutes until fragrant and golden brown.
   - Stir in the garam masala (if using), tomato paste, soy sauce, Worcestershire sauce, and sugar until well combined.

- Gradually whisk in the water or broth, stirring constantly to prevent lumps. Cook the mixture, stirring occasionally, until it thickens to the consistency of gravy. Remove from heat and set aside.
2. Cook the Vegetables and Protein:
    - Heat the vegetable oil in a large pot or Dutch oven over medium heat. Add the chopped onion and cook until softened and translucent, about 5 minutes.
    - Add the diced carrots, potatoes, and any other vegetables you're using, and cook for another 5 minutes, stirring occasionally.
    - Push the vegetables to one side of the pot and add the protein to the empty space. Cook until browned on all sides, about 5 minutes.
3. Simmer the Curry:
    - Pour the water or broth into the pot with the vegetables and protein. Bring the mixture to a boil, then reduce the heat to low and let it simmer for about 15-20 minutes, or until the vegetables are tender and the protein is cooked through.
4. Add the Curry Roux:
    - Once the vegetables and protein are cooked, add the Japanese curry roux to the pot. Stir well until the roux is fully dissolved and the curry thickens. Taste and adjust the seasoning with salt and pepper if needed.
5. Serve:
    - Serve the Japanese curry hot over cooked rice.
6. Enjoy!
    - Enjoy your homemade Japanese curry with rice and any desired toppings, such as fukujinzuke (pickled vegetables) or sliced boiled eggs. It's a comforting and satisfying meal that's perfect for any occasion!

Shabu-shabu hot pot

Ingredients:

For the Broth:

- 6 cups water
- 2 cups dashi stock (or substitute with chicken or vegetable broth)
- 2 tablespoons soy sauce
- 2 tablespoons mirin (Japanese sweet rice wine)
- 2 tablespoons sake (Japanese rice wine)
- 1 tablespoon sugar
- 2 cloves garlic, crushed (optional)
- 1-inch piece of ginger, sliced (optional)

For the Hot Pot Ingredients:

- Thinly sliced beef (such as ribeye or sirloin)
- Assorted vegetables (Napa cabbage, bok choy, spinach, mushrooms, carrots, green onions, etc.)
- Tofu (firm or silken), sliced
- Shirataki noodles or udon noodles (optional)
- Enoki or shiitake mushrooms
- Fish cakes or seafood (optional)
- Cooked rice or udon noodles for serving

For Dipping Sauces (optional):

- Ponzu sauce (citrusy soy sauce)
- Sesame sauce (ground sesame seeds mixed with soy sauce and sugar)
- Goma dare (creamy sesame sauce)
- Yuzu kosho (citrusy chili paste)

Instructions:

1. Prepare the Broth:

- In a large pot, combine water, dashi stock, soy sauce, mirin, sake, sugar, crushed garlic, and sliced ginger. Bring to a boil over medium heat, then reduce to a simmer. Let the broth simmer for about 15-20 minutes to infuse the flavors.
2. Prepare the Ingredients:
    - Arrange the thinly sliced beef, assorted vegetables, tofu, noodles, mushrooms, and other desired ingredients on plates or in bowls for easy access at the table.
3. Set Up the Table:
    - Place an electric or portable gas hot pot in the center of the dining table. If using a traditional pot, you can use a portable burner to keep the broth hot during the meal.
4. Cooking Process:
    - Once the broth is simmering, each diner can use chopsticks or a small ladle to place their desired ingredients into the hot pot to cook.
    - Dip the ingredients into the hot broth and cook until they are cooked to your liking. The thinly sliced meat cooks very quickly, often in just a few seconds.
    - Use chopsticks or a small strainer to remove the cooked ingredients from the pot and transfer them to individual plates.
5. Dipping Sauces:
    - Serve the dipping sauces in small bowls for each diner to customize their flavors. Ponzu sauce, sesame sauce, goma dare, and yuzu kosho are popular options.
6. Serving:
    - Serve the cooked ingredients with steamed rice or udon noodles on the side. You can also enjoy the hot pot broth as a soup at the end of the meal.
7. Enjoy!
    - Enjoy your homemade shabu-shabu hot pot with friends and family, dipping the cooked ingredients into your favorite sauces and savoring the delicious flavors. It's a fun and interactive dining experience that's perfect for gatherings and special occasions!

Oyakodon chicken and egg rice bowl

Ingredients:

- 2 boneless, skinless chicken thighs, thinly sliced
- 1 onion, thinly sliced
- 3 eggs
- 1 cup dashi stock (or substitute with chicken or vegetable broth)
- 3 tablespoons soy sauce
- 2 tablespoons mirin (Japanese sweet rice wine)
- 1 tablespoon sugar
- 2 cups cooked Japanese short-grain rice
- Chopped green onions, for garnish (optional)
- Nori (seaweed) flakes, for garnish (optional)

Instructions:

1. Prepare the Sauce:
    - In a small bowl, mix together the dashi stock, soy sauce, mirin, and sugar until well combined. Set aside.
2. Cook the Chicken and Onion:
    - Heat a large skillet or frying pan over medium heat. Add the sliced onion and cook until softened, about 3-4 minutes.
    - Add the sliced chicken to the skillet and cook until it is no longer pink, about 3-4 minutes.
3. Add the Sauce:
    - Pour the prepared sauce over the chicken and onion in the skillet. Bring the mixture to a simmer and let it cook for another 2-3 minutes, allowing the flavors to meld together.
4. Add the Eggs:
    - In a small bowl, beat the eggs until well mixed. Slowly pour the beaten eggs over the chicken and onion mixture in the skillet, evenly distributing them.
    - Cover the skillet with a lid and let the eggs cook until they are just set, about 2-3 minutes. Be careful not to overcook the eggs.
5. Assemble the Oyakodon:
    - Divide the cooked rice evenly among serving bowls.

- Using a spatula, carefully transfer the chicken, onion, and egg mixture from the skillet onto the rice in each bowl, ensuring that the eggs are evenly distributed.
6. Garnish and Serve:
    - Garnish each bowl of oyakodon with chopped green onions and nori flakes for extra flavor and visual appeal, if desired.
7. Enjoy!
    - Serve the oyakodon hot and enjoy the delicious combination of tender chicken, sweet onion, and savory egg over a bed of fluffy rice. It's a comforting and satisfying meal that's perfect for lunch or dinner!

Agedashi tofu

Ingredients:

For the Agedashi Tofu:

- 1 block (about 14 ounces) firm tofu
- Cornstarch or potato starch for coating
- Vegetable oil for frying

For the Dashi Broth:

- 2 cups dashi stock (Japanese soup stock, made from kombu seaweed and bonito flakes)
- 2 tablespoons soy sauce
- 2 tablespoons mirin (Japanese sweet rice wine)
- 1 tablespoon sake (Japanese rice wine)
- 1 teaspoon sugar

For Garnish:

- Grated daikon radish
- Grated ginger
- Thinly sliced green onions (scallions)
- Bonito flakes (katsuobushi)
- Shredded nori (seaweed)

Instructions:

1. Prepare the Tofu:
    - Drain the tofu and wrap it in paper towels or a clean kitchen towel. Place a heavy object on top (such as a plate or cutting board with a weight on top) to press out excess moisture. Let it press for about 20-30 minutes.
    - Once pressed, cut the tofu block into 8 equal pieces.
2. Coat and Fry the Tofu:
    - Heat vegetable oil in a deep skillet or saucepan to 350°F (180°C).

- Lightly coat each piece of tofu in cornstarch or potato starch, shaking off any excess.
- Carefully add the tofu to the hot oil and fry until golden brown and crispy, about 3-4 minutes per side. Work in batches if necessary to avoid overcrowding the pan.
- Once fried, transfer the tofu to a plate lined with paper towels to drain excess oil.

3. Prepare the Dashi Broth:
   - In a small saucepan, combine the dashi stock, soy sauce, mirin, sake, and sugar. Bring the mixture to a simmer over medium heat and let it cook for a few minutes to allow the flavors to meld together. Remove from heat.

4. Serve the Agedashi Tofu:
   - Arrange the fried tofu pieces in serving bowls or on a serving plate.
   - Ladle the hot dashi broth over the tofu until it is partially submerged.
   - Garnish each serving with grated daikon radish, grated ginger, thinly sliced green onions, bonito flakes, and shredded nori.

5. Enjoy!
   - Serve the agedashi tofu immediately while hot and enjoy the crispy texture of the tofu combined with the umami-rich dashi broth and refreshing garnishes. It makes a delicious and satisfying appetizer or side dish!

Katsu-don pork cutlet rice bowl

Ingredients:

For the Tonkatsu (Pork Cutlet):

- 4 boneless pork loin chops (about 1/2 inch thick)
- Salt and pepper
- All-purpose flour, for dredging
- 2 large eggs, beaten
- Panko breadcrumbs, for coating
- Vegetable oil, for frying

For the Sauce:

- 1/4 cup dashi stock (or substitute with chicken or vegetable broth)
- 2 tablespoons soy sauce
- 2 tablespoons mirin (Japanese sweet rice wine)
- 1 tablespoon sugar
- 1 onion, thinly sliced

For Serving:

- 4 cups cooked Japanese short-grain rice
- 4 eggs
- Chopped green onions, for garnish (optional)
- Pickled ginger (beni shoga), for garnish (optional)

Instructions:

1. Prepare the Tonkatsu:
    - Season the pork chops with salt and pepper on both sides.
    - Dredge each pork chop in flour, shaking off any excess.
    - Dip the floured pork chops into the beaten eggs, then coat them evenly with panko breadcrumbs, pressing gently to adhere.
    - Heat vegetable oil in a large skillet or frying pan over medium heat. Fry the pork chops until golden brown and crispy on both sides, about 4-5 minutes

per side. Transfer to a plate lined with paper towels to drain excess oil. Set aside.
2. Make the Sauce:
   - In a small saucepan, combine the dashi stock, soy sauce, mirin, and sugar. Bring the mixture to a simmer over medium heat.
   - Add the thinly sliced onion to the sauce and let it cook for about 5 minutes until softened.
3. Assemble the Katsudon:
   - Slice the cooked tonkatsu into strips or bite-sized pieces.
   - Divide the cooked rice among serving bowls.
   - Place the sliced tonkatsu on top of the rice in each bowl.
   - Spoon the simmered onion and sauce over the tonkatsu in each bowl.
4. Add the Egg Topping:
   - In a small bowl, beat one egg and pour it evenly over the tonkatsu and sauce in each bowl.
   - Cover the skillet with a lid and cook over low heat until the eggs are just set, about 2-3 minutes.
5. Garnish and Serve:
   - Garnish each bowl with chopped green onions and pickled ginger, if desired.
6. Enjoy!
   - Serve the katsudon hot and enjoy the delicious combination of crispy tonkatsu, savory sauce, and fluffy rice. It's a comforting and satisfying meal that's perfect for lunch or dinner!

Nikujaga beef and potato stew

Ingredients:

- 1 lb (450g) thinly sliced beef (such as beef chuck or ribeye)
- 2 large potatoes, peeled and cut into chunks
- 1 onion, thinly sliced
- 1 carrot, peeled and sliced into rounds
- 2 cups dashi stock (or substitute with beef, chicken, or vegetable broth)
- 3 tablespoons soy sauce
- 3 tablespoons mirin (Japanese sweet rice wine)
- 1 tablespoon sugar
- 1 tablespoon vegetable oil
- Salt and pepper to taste
- Green onions, thinly sliced (for garnish, optional)

Instructions:

1. Prepare the Ingredients:
    - Cut the beef into bite-sized pieces if they are not already thinly sliced.
    - Peel and chop the potatoes into large chunks.
    - Thinly slice the onion and peel and slice the carrot into rounds.
2. Cook the Beef:
    - Heat vegetable oil in a large pot or Dutch oven over medium heat.
    - Add the thinly sliced beef to the pot and cook until browned on all sides, about 3-4 minutes. Season with salt and pepper to taste.
3. Add the Vegetables:
    - Add the sliced onion and carrot rounds to the pot with the beef. Cook for another 2-3 minutes until the vegetables are slightly softened.
4. Make the Broth:
    - Pour the dashi stock (or broth) into the pot with the beef and vegetables.
    - Add the soy sauce, mirin, and sugar to the pot, stirring to combine.
5. Simmer:
    - Bring the mixture to a boil, then reduce the heat to low and let it simmer, covered, for about 10 minutes.
6. Add the Potatoes:

- Add the chopped potatoes to the pot with the beef and vegetables, ensuring they are submerged in the broth.
7. Continue to Cook:
   - Continue to simmer the nikujaga, covered, for another 15-20 minutes or until the potatoes are tender and cooked through. Stir occasionally to prevent sticking.
8. Adjust Seasoning:
   - Taste the nikujaga and adjust the seasoning with more soy sauce, mirin, sugar, salt, or pepper as needed to achieve the desired flavor balance.
9. Serve:
   - Once the potatoes are cooked through and the flavors have melded together, remove the pot from the heat.
   - Serve the nikujaga hot, garnished with thinly sliced green onions if desired.
10. Enjoy!
    - Enjoy your homemade nikujaga beef and potato stew as a comforting and satisfying meal, perfect for chilly days or any time you're craving a taste of Japanese home cooking!

Tamago egg sushi

Ingredients:

For the sweet egg mixture:

- 4 large eggs
- 2 tablespoons sugar
- 2 tablespoons mirin (sweet rice wine)
- 1 tablespoon soy sauce
- 1/4 teaspoon salt

For the sushi rice:

- 1 cup sushi rice
- 1 1/4 cups water
- 2 tablespoons rice vinegar
- 2 teaspoons sugar
- 1/2 teaspoon salt

For assembling the sushi:

- Nori (seaweed sheets), optional
- Soy sauce, for serving
- Wasabi, for serving
- Pickled ginger, for serving

Instructions:

1. Prepare the sushi rice:
    - Rinse the sushi rice in cold water until the water runs clear.
    - Combine the rinsed rice and water in a rice cooker or pot. Cook according to the rice cooker's instructions or bring to a boil, then reduce heat to low,

cover, and simmer for about 15-20 minutes until the rice is cooked and water is absorbed.
    - In a small bowl, mix the rice vinegar, sugar, and salt until dissolved. Gently fold this mixture into the cooked rice while it's still warm. Let the rice cool to room temperature.
2. Make the sweet egg mixture:
    - In a bowl, beat the eggs well.
    - Add sugar, mirin, soy sauce, and salt to the beaten eggs. Mix until well combined.
    - Strain the mixture through a fine mesh sieve to remove any lumps.
3. Cook the egg:
    - Heat a non-stick frying pan over medium heat. Lightly grease the pan with oil or butter.
    - Pour a thin layer of the egg mixture into the pan, just enough to cover the bottom.
    - Once the bottom layer is set but still slightly runny on top, gently roll it up from one side of the pan to the other using a spatula or chopsticks.
    - Push the rolled egg to the opposite side of the pan, then grease the empty side lightly before pouring more egg mixture to form another layer.
    - Repeat the rolling and layering process until all the egg mixture is used up. Remove the rolled egg from the pan and let it cool.
4. Assemble the sushi:
    - Cut the rolled egg into rectangular slices, about the same size as your sushi rice.
    - Take a small amount of sushi rice and form it into an oval shape.
    - Place a slice of the rolled egg on top of the rice, gently pressing it down to adhere.
    - Optionally, you can wrap a strip of nori around the sushi to hold it together.
    - Repeat the process until all the sushi rice and egg slices are used up.
5. Serve:
    - Arrange the tamago sushi on a serving plate.
    - Serve with soy sauce, wasabi, and pickled ginger on the side.

Enjoy your homemade tamago sushi! Feel free to adjust the sweetness or seasoning according to your taste preferences.

Chawanmushi savory egg custard

Ingredients:

- 2 cups dashi (Japanese soup stock) - you can make your own dashi or use instant dashi granules
- 4 large eggs
- 1 tablespoon soy sauce
- 1 tablespoon mirin (sweet rice wine)
- 1/2 teaspoon salt
- Optional toppings (choose from shrimp, chicken, mushrooms, kamaboko - fish cake, ginkgo nuts, green peas, etc.)

Instructions:

1. Prepare the ingredients:
    - If you're using homemade dashi, prepare it according to your preferred method. If using instant dashi, dissolve the granules in hot water according to the package instructions.
    - Prepare your choice of toppings by cooking them separately. For example, if using shrimp or chicken, you can lightly sauté or poach them until cooked. Slice mushrooms and kamaboko thinly. Blanch ginkgo nuts if using.
2. Make the chawanmushi base:
    - In a mixing bowl, beat the eggs gently until well combined.
    - Gradually pour in the dashi while continuing to whisk the eggs.
    - Add soy sauce, mirin, and salt to the egg mixture. Stir until everything is evenly incorporated.
3. Assemble the chawanmushi:
    - Divide your choice of toppings among the serving cups or bowls. Make sure they're evenly distributed.
    - Pour the egg mixture over the toppings, filling each cup or bowl about 3/4 full. You can strain the mixture through a fine sieve to achieve a smoother texture if desired.
4. Steam the chawanmushi:
    - Prepare a steamer large enough to accommodate the cups or bowls. If you don't have a steamer, you can use a large pot with a rack or a makeshift steaming setup.

- Once the water in the steamer is boiling, carefully place the cups or bowls in the steamer basket.
- Cover the steamer with a lid and steam the chawanmushi over medium-low heat for about 15-20 minutes, or until the custard is set but still slightly jiggly in the center.

5. Serve:
    - Carefully remove the chawanmushi from the steamer.
    - Serve the custards hot, either directly in the cups or bowls they were steamed in, or transfer them to serving plates.
    - Garnish with additional toppings if desired, such as a sprinkle of chopped green onions or a small dollop of grated ginger.
    - Enjoy your homemade chawanmushi as a comforting and flavorful appetizer or side dish!

Feel free to adjust the ingredients and toppings according to your taste preferences. Chawanmushi is versatile, so you can get creative with your favorite ingredients.

Sunomono cucumber salad

Ingredients:

- 2 medium cucumbers
- 1/4 cup rice vinegar
- 2 tablespoons sugar
- 1 tablespoon soy sauce
- 1/2 teaspoon salt
- 1 teaspoon sesame seeds (optional)
- Thinly sliced seaweed (such as nori) for garnish (optional)

Instructions:

1. Prepare the cucumbers:
    - Wash the cucumbers thoroughly under cold water.
    - Optionally, you can peel the cucumbers if desired, but leaving the skin on adds color and texture to the salad.
    - Slice the cucumbers thinly into rounds. You can also use a mandoline slicer for evenly thin slices.
2. Make the dressing:
    - In a small bowl, combine the rice vinegar, sugar, soy sauce, and salt. Stir until the sugar and salt are completely dissolved.
3. Marinate the cucumbers:
    - Place the sliced cucumbers in a large bowl.
    - Pour the dressing over the cucumbers, making sure they are evenly coated.
    - Gently toss the cucumbers to ensure they're well-marinated in the dressing.
    - Cover the bowl with plastic wrap or a lid and refrigerate for at least 30 minutes to allow the flavors to meld together. You can refrigerate for longer if you prefer a more intensely flavored salad.
4. Serve:
    - Before serving, give the cucumber salad a quick toss.
    - Sprinkle sesame seeds over the salad for added flavor and texture, if desired.
    - Optionally, garnish with thinly sliced seaweed (nori) for a traditional touch.

- Serve the sunomono cucumber salad chilled as a refreshing side dish or appetizer.

Enjoy your homemade sunomono cucumber salad! It's perfect for hot summer days or as a light and healthy addition to any Japanese meal. Feel free to adjust the sweetness or tartness of the dressing to suit your taste preferences.

Anmitsu fruit jelly dessert

Ingredients:

For the agar jelly:

- 1 packet (7g) agar agar powder or 1 tablespoon agar agar flakes
- 4 cups water
- 1/2 cup sugar

For the toppings:

- Sweet azuki bean paste (anko), store-bought or homemade
- Assorted fruits such as strawberries, kiwi, oranges, and canned fruit cocktail
- Kuromitsu (brown sugar syrup), store-bought or homemade
- Optional: shiratama dango (rice flour dumplings) or mochi balls

Instructions:

1. Prepare the agar jelly:
    - In a saucepan, combine the agar agar powder or flakes with water. Let it sit for about 10 minutes to soften.
    - Place the saucepan over medium heat and bring the mixture to a boil, stirring occasionally to dissolve the agar agar completely.
    - Once boiling, reduce the heat to low and simmer for about 2-3 minutes.
    - Add sugar to the mixture and stir until dissolved.
    - Remove the saucepan from the heat and let the agar jelly mixture cool slightly.
2. Pour and set the jelly:
    - Pour the agar jelly mixture into a shallow dish or square baking pan.
    - Let it cool to room temperature, then refrigerate for at least 1-2 hours, or until the jelly is completely set.
3. Prepare the toppings:
    - Cut the assorted fruits into bite-sized pieces. If using canned fruit cocktail, drain the fruit well.
    - If desired, prepare shiratama dango or mochi balls according to the package instructions.

4. Assemble the Anmitsu:
    - Once the agar jelly is set, use a knife to cut it into small cubes.
    - Divide the agar jelly cubes among serving bowls or glasses.
    - Top the jelly cubes with a spoonful of sweet azuki bean paste (anko) and the assorted fruits.
    - If using, add shiratama dango or mochi balls to the bowls.
    - Drizzle kuromitsu (brown sugar syrup) over the Anmitsu as a sweet finishing touch.
5. Serve:
    - Serve the Anmitsu fruit jelly dessert immediately, either chilled or at room temperature.
    - Enjoy the refreshing combination of textures and flavors!

Feel free to customize your Anmitsu with your favorite fruits and toppings. It's a versatile dessert that's sure to please any palate, and it's perfect for special occasions or as a sweet treat any day of the week.

Yaki soba fried noodles

Ingredients:

- 200g yakisoba noodles (or substitute with ramen noodles or spaghetti)
- 1 tablespoon vegetable oil
- 1 small onion, thinly sliced
- 1 small carrot, julienned
- 1 small bell pepper, thinly sliced
- 1 cup cabbage, thinly sliced
- 2 cloves garlic, minced
- 100g thinly sliced pork belly, chicken, or shrimp (optional)
- 2 tablespoons soy sauce
- 1 tablespoon oyster sauce
- 1 tablespoon Worcestershire sauce
- 1 tablespoon ketchup
- 1 tablespoon sake or dry sherry (optional)
- Salt and pepper to taste
- Toasted sesame seeds and chopped green onions for garnish (optional)

Instructions:

1. Prepare the noodles:
    - If using fresh yakisoba noodles, follow the package instructions to cook them until al dente. If using dried noodles, cook them according to the package instructions, then rinse under cold water and drain well.
    - If using yakisoba noodles, they may come pre-cooked and vacuum-sealed. In this case, you can briefly rinse them under hot water to loosen them up, then drain well.
2. Prepare the sauce:
    - In a small bowl, mix together the soy sauce, oyster sauce, Worcestershire sauce, ketchup, and sake or dry sherry (if using). Set aside.
3. Stir-fry the vegetables and protein:
    - Heat the vegetable oil in a large skillet or wok over medium-high heat.
    - Add the sliced onion, carrot, bell pepper, and cabbage to the skillet. Stir-fry for 2-3 minutes until the vegetables start to soften.

- Add the minced garlic and thinly sliced meat or seafood (if using) to the skillet. Stir-fry for an additional 2-3 minutes until the meat is cooked through.
4. Add the noodles and sauce:
    - Add the cooked noodles to the skillet, using tongs to separate and loosen them if they're stuck together.
    - Pour the prepared sauce over the noodles and vegetables in the skillet.
    - Toss everything together until the noodles are evenly coated in the sauce and heated through. This should take about 2-3 minutes.
5. Season and garnish:
    - Taste the yakisoba and adjust the seasoning with salt and pepper if needed.
    - Transfer the yakisoba to serving plates or bowls.
    - Garnish with toasted sesame seeds and chopped green onions, if desired.
6. Serve:
    - Serve the yaki soba fried noodles immediately while hot.
    - Enjoy this delicious and flavorful Japanese stir-fried noodle dish as a satisfying meal any time of the day!

Feel free to customize your yaki soba with your favorite vegetables and protein options. It's a versatile dish that can be adapted to suit your taste preferences.

Hiyayakko cold tofu

Ingredients:

- 1 block (about 14 oz or 400g) of firm or silken tofu
- Soy sauce, for drizzling
- Optional toppings: grated ginger, thinly sliced green onions, bonito flakes (katsuobushi), sesame seeds, shredded nori seaweed

Instructions:

1. Prepare the tofu:
    - Remove the tofu from its packaging and drain any excess water.
    - If using firm tofu, you can slice it into cubes or rectangles. If using silken tofu, you may prefer to serve it in its original form without slicing.
2. Plate the tofu:
    - Arrange the tofu slices or blocks on serving plates or a shallow dish, making sure they're evenly spaced.
3. Add toppings:
    - Drizzle soy sauce over the tofu slices or blocks, using as much or as little as you like.
    - Optionally, sprinkle grated ginger, thinly sliced green onions, bonito flakes (katsuobushi), sesame seeds, or shredded nori seaweed over the tofu for added flavor and texture.
4. Serve:
    - Serve the hiyayakko immediately as a refreshing appetizer or side dish.
    - Enjoy the creamy texture and delicate flavor of the cold tofu, complemented by the savory soy sauce and toppings.

Feel free to customize your hiyayakko with your favorite toppings or additional seasonings, such as a drizzle of sesame oil or a splash of rice vinegar. It's a versatile dish that you can adjust to suit your taste preferences.

Zaru soba cold buckwheat noodles

Ingredients:

For the soba noodles:

- 8 ounces (about 225g) dried soba noodles
- Water for boiling

For the dipping sauce (Tsuyu):

- 1 cup dashi (Japanese soup stock)
- 1/4 cup soy sauce
- 1/4 cup mirin (sweet rice wine)
- 1 tablespoon sugar
- Optional: grated daikon radish and sliced green onions for garnish

For serving:

- Nori (seaweed sheets), cut into thin strips
- Wasabi (Japanese horseradish paste)
- Grated ginger (optional)

Instructions:

1. Cook the soba noodles:
    - Bring a large pot of water to a boil.
    - Add the soba noodles to the boiling water and cook according to the package instructions, usually about 5-7 minutes, or until the noodles are tender but still slightly firm (al dente).
    - Stir the noodles occasionally to prevent sticking.
    - Once cooked, drain the noodles in a colander and rinse them under cold running water to remove excess starch and stop the cooking process.
    - Shake off any excess water and set the noodles aside.

2. Prepare the dipping sauce (Tsuyu):
   - In a saucepan, combine the dashi, soy sauce, mirin, and sugar.
   - Bring the mixture to a gentle simmer over medium heat, stirring occasionally to dissolve the sugar.
   - Once the sugar is dissolved and the flavors have melded together, remove the saucepan from the heat and let the dipping sauce cool to room temperature.
3. Prepare the toppings:
   - If using, grate the daikon radish and slice the green onions thinly.
   - Cut the nori (seaweed sheets) into thin strips.
4. Serve the Zaru Soba:
   - Divide the cooked soba noodles among serving plates or bamboo baskets (traditionally used for serving Zaru Soba).
   - Optionally, garnish the noodles with grated daikon radish and sliced green onions.
   - Arrange the nori strips on the side of the plates or baskets.
   - Serve wasabi and grated ginger on small plates or bowls alongside the noodles.
5. Enjoy:
   - To eat, take a portion of the chilled soba noodles with your chopsticks and dip them into the dipping sauce (Tsuyu) along with a small amount of wasabi and grated ginger, if desired.
   - Enjoy the refreshing and savory flavors of Zaru Soba, and feel free to slurp the noodles as is customary in Japanese dining etiquette!

Zaru Soba is a versatile dish, and you can customize it with additional toppings such as tempura shrimp or vegetables, sliced cucumber, or shredded nori seaweed. It's a delicious and healthy meal that's perfect for hot summer days.

Dango sweet dumplings

Ingredients:

For the dango dough:

- 1 cup glutinous rice flour (mochiko)
- 1/4 cup water (plus more as needed)
- Optional: food coloring or flavorings such as matcha powder or sakura (cherry blossom) extract

For the toppings (optional):

- Sweet soy sauce (mitarashi sauce)
- Kinako (roasted soybean flour)
- White or black sesame seeds
- Shredded coconut
- Anko (sweet red bean paste)
- Matcha powder

Instructions:

1. Prepare the dango dough:
    - In a mixing bowl, combine the glutinous rice flour with water and mix well until a smooth, elastic dough forms. Add more water if needed to achieve the right consistency.
    - If you're adding food coloring or flavorings, knead them into the dough until evenly distributed.
2. Shape the dango:
    - Divide the dough into small portions and roll each portion into a ball, about 1 inch (2.5 cm) in diameter.
    - Optionally, you can flatten each ball slightly to create a disc-shaped dumpling, or leave them round.
3. Cook the dango:
    - Bring a pot of water to a boil.
    - Carefully drop the dango balls into the boiling water, a few at a time, making sure they don't stick together.

- Cook the dango for about 2-3 minutes, or until they float to the surface and become slightly translucent.
- Using a slotted spoon, transfer the cooked dango to a bowl of cold water to stop the cooking process and firm up the texture.
- Drain the dango and thread them onto skewers, if desired.

4. Add toppings (optional):
    - Dip the skewered dango into sweet soy sauce (mitarashi sauce) for a savory-sweet flavor, or roll them in kinako (roasted soybean flour) for a nutty taste.
    - You can also sprinkle the dango with sesame seeds, shredded coconut, or matcha powder for additional flavor and texture.
    - Alternatively, serve the dango with a side of anko (sweet red bean paste) for dipping.
5. Serve:
    - Arrange the dango skewers on a serving plate or platter.
    - Enjoy the sweet dumplings as a delightful snack or dessert, either warm or chilled.

Dango is a versatile treat, and you can experiment with different toppings and flavorings to create your own unique variations. Whether enjoyed on their own or as part of a larger spread, dango sweet dumplings are sure to satisfy your sweet tooth!

Mochi rice cakes

Ingredients:

- 1 cup glutinous rice flour (mochiko)
- 1/2 cup granulated sugar
- 3/4 cup water
- Potato starch or cornstarch, for dusting
- Optional fillings or toppings: sweet red bean paste (anko), kinako (roasted soybean flour), sesame seeds, fruit preserves, etc.

Instructions:

1. Prepare the mochi dough:
    - In a microwave-safe bowl, combine the glutinous rice flour and sugar.
    - Gradually add the water to the flour mixture, stirring until smooth and well combined.
2. Microwave the mochi dough:
    - Cover the bowl loosely with plastic wrap to prevent splattering.
    - Microwave the dough on high for 1 minute.
3. Knead the mochi dough:
    - Carefully remove the bowl from the microwave and stir the dough with a spatula.
    - The dough will be hot and sticky, so use caution.
    - Return the dough to the microwave and cook for an additional 1 minute.
4. Shape the mochi:
    - Dust a clean work surface with potato starch or cornstarch to prevent sticking.
    - Transfer the hot mochi dough to the dusted surface.
    - Use a spatula or spoon to flatten and spread out the dough into a thin layer, about 1/4 inch (6 mm) thick.
5. Cut and fill the mochi (optional):
    - If desired, cut the flattened mochi dough into small squares or circles using a knife or cookie cutter.
    - Place a small amount of your chosen filling (such as sweet red bean paste) in the center of each piece of mochi.
6. Fold and seal the mochi:
    - Carefully lift the edges of the mochi dough to enclose the filling.

- Pinch the edges together to seal the mochi, forming small parcels or balls.
7. Dust with starch:
    - Dust the finished mochi rice cakes with additional potato starch or cornstarch to prevent sticking.
8. Serve or store:
    - Serve the mochi rice cakes immediately as a sweet snack or dessert.
    - Alternatively, store the mochi in an airtight container in the refrigerator for up to a few days. Mochi is best enjoyed fresh, but it can be reheated briefly in the microwave to soften if needed.

Mochi rice cakes are a versatile treat, and you can customize them with various fillings and toppings to suit your taste preferences. Experiment with different flavors and enjoy the chewy goodness of homemade mochi!

Omurice omelette rice

Ingredients:

For the fried rice:

- 2 cups cooked Japanese short-grain rice (preferably leftover rice)
- 1 tablespoon vegetable oil
- 1/2 onion, finely chopped
- 1 small carrot, finely diced
- 1/2 cup frozen peas
- 2 tablespoons ketchup
- Salt and pepper to taste

For the omelette:

- 4 large eggs
- 2 tablespoons milk or water
- Salt and pepper to taste
- 1 tablespoon butter

For garnish (optional):

- Additional ketchup
- Chopped green onions
- Toasted sesame seeds

Instructions:

1. Prepare the fried rice:
    - Heat the vegetable oil in a large skillet or wok over medium heat.
    - Add the chopped onion and diced carrot to the skillet. Stir-fry for 2-3 minutes until the vegetables start to soften.

- Add the frozen peas to the skillet and continue to stir-fry for another 1-2 minutes.
- Add the cooked rice to the skillet, breaking up any clumps with a spatula.
- Drizzle the ketchup over the rice and vegetables. Stir well to coat everything evenly.
- Season the fried rice with salt and pepper to taste. Cook for another 2-3 minutes, stirring occasionally, until the rice is heated through and lightly golden. Remove from heat and set aside.

2. Make the omelette:
    - In a mixing bowl, beat the eggs with milk or water until well combined.
    - Season the egg mixture with salt and pepper to taste.
    - Heat the butter in a non-stick skillet over medium-low heat.
    - Pour the beaten eggs into the skillet and let them cook undisturbed for a minute or until the edges start to set.
3. Assemble the omurice:
    - Once the edges of the omelette start to set, gently push them towards the center of the skillet with a spatula, allowing the uncooked eggs to flow to the edges.
    - Continue to cook the omelette until it's mostly set but still slightly runny on top.
4. Add the fried rice:
    - Spoon the fried rice onto one half of the omelette in the skillet.
5. Fold and serve:
    - Using a spatula, carefully fold the other half of the omelette over the fried rice to enclose it completely.
    - Slide the omurice onto a serving plate, ensuring that the omelette is folded neatly over the rice.
    - Optionally, drizzle additional ketchup over the top of the omurice and garnish with chopped green onions and toasted sesame seeds.
6. Serve immediately:
    - Enjoy your homemade omurice while it's hot, cutting into it to reveal the fluffy scrambled eggs and flavorful fried rice inside.

Omurice is a versatile dish, and you can customize it by adding other ingredients such as diced chicken, ham, mushrooms, or bell peppers to the fried rice. It's a comforting and satisfying meal that's perfect for lunch or dinner!

Nabemono hot pot dishes

Ingredients:

For the broth:

- 6 cups dashi stock (you can use instant dashi granules or make your own)
- 1/4 cup soy sauce
- 1/4 cup mirin
- 2 tablespoons sake (Japanese rice wine)
- 1 tablespoon sugar

For the hot pot:

- 8 ounces firm tofu, cut into cubes
- 8 ounces boneless, skinless chicken thighs or breast, thinly sliced
- 8 ounces shrimp, peeled and deveined
- 4 shiitake mushrooms, stems removed and sliced
- 1 cup Napa cabbage, sliced
- 1 carrot, peeled and thinly sliced
- 1/2 block konnyaku (yam cake), sliced (optional)
- 4 green onions, cut into 2-inch pieces
- 4 shirataki noodles (yam noodles), rinsed and drained (optional)
- 1/4 cup mizuna or spinach leaves (optional)
- Additional toppings: enoki mushrooms, fish balls, kamaboko (fish cake), etc.

For dipping sauce (Ponzu):

- 1/4 cup soy sauce
- 2 tablespoons lemon juice or rice vinegar
- 1 tablespoon mirin
- 1 tablespoon dashi stock

Instructions:

1. Prepare the broth:

- In a large pot, combine the dashi stock, soy sauce, mirin, sake, and sugar. Bring to a simmer over medium heat and let it cook for about 5 minutes to allow the flavors to meld together. Adjust the seasoning if needed.

2. Prepare the hot pot ingredients:
   - Arrange the tofu, chicken, shrimp, shiitake mushrooms, Napa cabbage, carrot, konnyaku, green onions, shirataki noodles, and mizuna or spinach in separate plates or bowls for easy access.
3. Set up the hot pot:
   - Place a portable gas burner or electric hot plate in the center of the dining table. Set a large nabe pot (Japanese hot pot) or a regular pot on the burner.
   - Pour the prepared broth into the pot and bring it to a gentle simmer over medium heat.
4. Cook the ingredients:
   - Start by adding the ingredients that take the longest to cook, such as chicken and root vegetables, to the simmering broth. Cook for a few minutes until they start to soften.
   - Gradually add the remaining ingredients to the pot, cooking each one until they're tender and cooked through. Be careful not to overcrowd the pot.
5. Make the dipping sauce (Ponzu):
   - In a small bowl, mix together the soy sauce, lemon juice or rice vinegar, mirin, and dashi stock to make the dipping sauce. Adjust the proportions to your taste preference.
6. Serve:
   - Once all the ingredients are cooked, turn off the heat and let the hot pot sit for a minute.
   - Ladle the cooked ingredients and broth into individual bowls or serve directly from the pot.
   - Serve the dipping sauce (Ponzu) on the side for dipping the cooked ingredients.
7. Enjoy:
   - Enjoy your homemade Yosenabe hot pot with friends and family, dipping the cooked ingredients into the flavorful Ponzu sauce before eating.

Feel free to customize your Yosenabe hot pot by adding your favorite ingredients or adjusting the seasoning to your taste preferences. It's a warm and comforting dish that's perfect for sharing on cold days!

Taiyaki fish-shaped cakes

Ingredients:

For the batter:

- 1 cup all-purpose flour
- 1 tablespoon cornstarch
- 1/4 teaspoon baking powder
- 1/4 cup granulated sugar
- 1 large egg
- 3/4 cup milk
- 1 tablespoon melted butter or vegetable oil

For the filling:

- Sweet red bean paste (anko), custard, chocolate spread, or any filling of your choice

Instructions:

1. Prepare the batter:
    - In a mixing bowl, sift together the all-purpose flour, cornstarch, baking powder, and granulated sugar.
    - In a separate bowl, whisk the egg and then add the milk and melted butter or vegetable oil. Mix until well combined.
    - Gradually add the wet ingredients to the dry ingredients, stirring until you have a smooth batter. Be careful not to overmix.
    - Cover the bowl with plastic wrap and let the batter rest in the refrigerator for about 30 minutes.
2. Preheat the taiyaki maker:
    - If you have a taiyaki maker, preheat it according to the manufacturer's instructions. If you don't have a taiyaki maker, you can use a special taiyaki pan or a regular waffle maker.
3. Fill the taiyaki:
    - Once the batter has rested, lightly grease the taiyaki molds with vegetable oil or non-stick cooking spray.
    - Pour a small amount of batter into each mold, filling it about halfway.

- Add a spoonful of your chosen filling (such as sweet red bean paste) on top of the batter in each mold, making sure not to overfill.
4. Cook the taiyaki:
    - Close the taiyaki maker or pan and cook the taiyaki for a few minutes until they're golden brown and crispy on the outside.
    - If using a taiyaki maker, flip it halfway through the cooking process to ensure even browning on both sides.
    - If using a taiyaki pan, flip the taiyaki using a spatula halfway through cooking.
5. Serve:
    - Once the taiyaki are cooked to your liking, carefully remove them from the maker or pan and transfer them to a wire rack to cool slightly.
    - Serve the taiyaki warm, either as is or dusted with powdered sugar for an extra touch of sweetness.
6. Enjoy:
    - Enjoy your homemade taiyaki as a delightful and nostalgic treat! They're best enjoyed fresh, but you can also store any leftovers in an airtight container at room temperature for a day or two.

Feel free to get creative with your taiyaki fillings. Besides the traditional red bean paste, custard, or chocolate, you can experiment with Nutella, matcha custard, sweet potato, or even savory fillings like cheese and ham. Let your imagination run wild!

Dorayaki red bean pancakes

Ingredients:

For the dorayaki pancakes:

- 2 large eggs
- 1/2 cup granulated sugar
- 1 tablespoon honey or maple syrup
- 1 teaspoon vanilla extract
- 1 cup all-purpose flour
- 1 teaspoon baking powder
- 2-3 tablespoons water, as needed
- Vegetable oil, for cooking

For the red bean paste filling (anko):

- 1 cup sweetened red bean paste (store-bought or homemade)

Instructions:

1. Make the red bean paste filling (anko):
    - If using store-bought red bean paste, skip to the next step. If making homemade red bean paste, you can find recipes online or use canned sweetened red bean paste.
    - Measure out 1 cup of red bean paste and set it aside.
2. Prepare the dorayaki batter:
    - In a mixing bowl, beat the eggs with granulated sugar until pale and fluffy.
    - Add the honey or maple syrup and vanilla extract to the egg mixture and mix until combined.
    - Sift the all-purpose flour and baking powder into the bowl with the egg mixture. Gently fold the dry ingredients into the wet ingredients until just combined. Be careful not to overmix.
    - If the batter is too thick, gradually add water, 1 tablespoon at a time, until you achieve a smooth and pourable consistency. The batter should be thick but still easily spreadable.
3. Cook the dorayaki pancakes:

- Heat a non-stick skillet or griddle over medium heat. Lightly grease the skillet with vegetable oil.
- Pour about 1/4 cup of the dorayaki batter onto the skillet, using a spoon or ladle to spread it into a circular shape, about 4 inches (10 cm) in diameter.
- Cook the pancakes for 1-2 minutes, or until bubbles start to form on the surface and the edges look set.
- Flip the pancakes and cook for an additional 1-2 minutes on the other side, or until golden brown and cooked through.
- Transfer the cooked pancakes to a plate and cover them with a clean kitchen towel to keep them warm while you cook the remaining pancakes.

4. Assemble the dorayaki:
   - Once all the pancakes are cooked, place one pancake flat-side up on a clean surface.
   - Spread a generous amount of red bean paste filling (anko) onto the center of the pancake, leaving a small border around the edges.
   - Place another pancake flat-side down on top of the filling to create a sandwich.

5. Serve:
   - Serve the dorayaki immediately as a delicious and comforting Japanese dessert.
   - You can enjoy dorayaki warm or at room temperature. They're perfect for snacking or as a sweet treat with a cup of tea or coffee.

Feel free to customize your dorayaki by using different fillings such as Nutella, custard, fruit preserves, or whipped cream. Enjoy experimenting with flavors and creating your own unique dorayaki creations!

Somen noodles with dipping sauce

Ingredients:

For the dipping sauce (Tsuyu):

- 2 cups dashi stock (you can use instant dashi granules or make your own)
- 1/2 cup soy sauce
- 1/4 cup mirin (Japanese sweet rice wine)
- 2 tablespoons sugar
- Optional: 1 tablespoon sake (Japanese rice wine)

For the somen noodles:

- 8 ounces somen noodles
- Ice cubes
- Optional toppings: thinly sliced green onions, grated ginger, shredded nori seaweed, wasabi

Instructions:

1. Prepare the dipping sauce (Tsuyu):
    - In a saucepan, combine the dashi stock, soy sauce, mirin, sugar, and sake (if using).
    - Bring the mixture to a simmer over medium heat, stirring occasionally to dissolve the sugar.
    - Once the sugar is dissolved and the flavors have melded together, remove the saucepan from the heat and let the dipping sauce cool to room temperature.
    - Transfer the dipping sauce to a serving bowl or individual dipping bowls.
2. Cook the somen noodles:
    - Bring a large pot of water to a boil.
    - Add the somen noodles to the boiling water and cook according to the package instructions, usually 2-3 minutes or until the noodles are tender but still slightly firm (al dente).

- While the noodles are cooking, prepare a large bowl of ice water.
- Once the noodles are cooked, immediately drain them and rinse under cold running water to stop the cooking process and cool them down quickly.
- Transfer the cooled noodles to the bowl of ice water and let them chill for a few minutes.
- Drain the chilled noodles well and divide them among serving plates or bowls.

3. Serve:
    - Serve the chilled somen noodles alongside the dipping sauce.
    - Optionally, garnish the noodles with thinly sliced green onions, grated ginger, shredded nori seaweed, or a small dollop of wasabi.
    - To eat, simply take a portion of the chilled somen noodles with your chopsticks and dip them into the dipping sauce. Enjoy the refreshing and savory flavors of the somen noodles with the flavorful dipping sauce.

Somen noodles with dipping sauce is a light and refreshing dish that's perfect for a summer meal or as a refreshing appetizer. Feel free to adjust the seasoning of the dipping sauce to your taste preferences and experiment with different toppings to add variety to the dish. Enjoy!

Yudofu hot tofu

Ingredients:

- 1 block (about 14 oz or 400g) firm tofu
- 4 cups water
- 1 piece kombu (dried kelp), about 4x4 inches (10x10 cm) in size
- Soy sauce, for dipping (optional)
- Grated ginger, for garnish (optional)
- Thinly sliced green onions, for garnish (optional)

Instructions:

1. Prepare the kombu broth:
    - In a large pot, combine the water and kombu. Let the kombu soak in the water for at least 30 minutes to infuse the broth with its flavor.
    - After soaking, place the pot over medium heat and slowly bring the water to a gentle simmer. Be careful not to let it boil, as boiling can make the broth bitter.
2. Prepare the tofu:
    - While the broth is heating, cut the tofu into cubes or slices, whichever you prefer. You can cut it into large cubes for a more rustic presentation or into smaller slices for quicker cooking.
    - If you prefer a softer texture, you can also briefly blanch the tofu in boiling water before adding it to the broth. This helps to remove excess moisture and gives the tofu a creamier texture.
3. Add the tofu to the broth:
    - Once the broth is simmering, carefully add the tofu to the pot.
    - Let the tofu simmer gently in the broth for about 10-15 minutes, or until heated through and infused with the flavors of the kombu.
4. Serve:
    - Once the tofu is heated through, remove the pot from the heat.
    - Using a slotted spoon, transfer the tofu cubes or slices to individual serving bowls.
    - Optionally, you can strain the broth and pour it over the tofu before serving, or you can serve the tofu with the broth on the side for dipping.

- Garnish the yudofu with grated ginger and thinly sliced green onions, if desired.
- Serve the yudofu hot as a comforting and nourishing dish.

Yudofu is often served with a simple dipping sauce made from soy sauce, grated ginger, and thinly sliced green onions. To enjoy, simply dip the tofu into the sauce before eating. It's a humble yet satisfying dish that highlights the natural flavor and texture of tofu.

Mitarashi dango grilled skewered dumplings

Ingredients:

For the dango:

- 1 cup mochiko (glutinous rice flour)
- 1/2 cup water

For the mitarashi sauce:

- 3 tablespoons soy sauce
- 2 tablespoons sugar
- 1 tablespoon mirin (Japanese sweet rice wine)
- 1/2 cup water
- 1 tablespoon potato starch or cornstarch mixed with 1 tablespoon water (optional, for thickening)

Instructions:

1. In a mixing bowl, combine the mochiko and water to form a smooth dough. If the dough is too dry, add a little more water; if it's too wet, add a bit more mochiko.
2. Divide the dough into equal-sized pieces and roll each piece into a small ball, about 1 inch in diameter.
3. Thread 3-4 balls onto each bamboo skewer, leaving a little space between each one.
4. In a small saucepan, combine the soy sauce, sugar, mirin, and water for the mitarashi sauce. Bring to a simmer over medium heat, stirring occasionally until the sugar is dissolved.
5. Once the sugar is dissolved, reduce the heat to low and let the sauce simmer for about 5-7 minutes, until it thickens slightly. If you prefer a thicker sauce, you can add the potato starch or cornstarch mixture and stir until the sauce thickens to your desired consistency.
6. Preheat a grill or grill pan over medium heat. Grill the skewered dango for 3-4 minutes on each side, or until lightly browned and cooked through.

7. Once the dango are cooked, brush them generously with the mitarashi sauce, making sure to coat them evenly.
8. Serve the mitarashi dango warm, either on the skewers or removed from the skewers and arranged on a plate. Enjoy!

This recipe makes about 12-16 mitarashi dango, depending on the size of the dumplings. Adjust the quantities as needed to make more or fewer servings.

Hōtō miso soup with flat noodles

Ingredients:

For the soup:

- 4 cups dashi stock (you can use instant dashi granules or make your own)
- 2 tablespoons miso paste (white or red, depending on your preference)
- 1 cup sliced mushrooms (shiitake, button, or your choice)
- 1 cup sliced carrots
- 1 cup chopped cabbage
- 1 cup chopped spinach
- 2 green onions, thinly sliced
- 1 tablespoon soy sauce (optional, for additional flavor)
- Salt and pepper to taste

For the noodles:

- 8 oz flat udon noodles (you can also use hōtō noodles if available)

Instructions:

1. In a large pot, bring the dashi stock to a simmer over medium heat.
2. Add the sliced mushrooms, carrots, and cabbage to the pot. Let the vegetables simmer for about 5-7 minutes, or until they start to soften.
3. While the vegetables are simmering, cook the flat udon noodles according to the package instructions. Once cooked, drain the noodles and set them aside.
4. Once the vegetables are tender, add the chopped spinach to the pot and let it wilt for a minute or two.
5. In a small bowl, mix the miso paste with a few tablespoons of hot broth from the pot to dissolve it and create a smooth mixture.
6. Add the dissolved miso paste to the pot and stir well to combine. Let the soup simmer gently for another 2-3 minutes, but do not let it boil, as boiling can diminish the flavor of the miso.

7. Taste the soup and adjust the seasoning with soy sauce, salt, and pepper as needed.
8. To serve, divide the cooked flat udon noodles into bowls and ladle the hot soup over the noodles. Garnish each bowl with sliced green onions.
9. Serve the Hōtō Miso Soup hot and enjoy its comforting flavors!

Feel free to customize this recipe by adding other vegetables or protein such as tofu, sliced cooked chicken, or seafood according to your preferences.

Chikuwa fish cakes

Ingredients:

- 300g white fish fillets (cod, pollock, or similar)
- 2 tablespoons potato starch or cornstarch
- 1 teaspoon salt
- 1 teaspoon sugar
- 1 tablespoon mirin (Japanese sweet rice wine)
- 1 tablespoon soy sauce
- Bamboo skewers, soaked in water (if grilling)
- Optional: nori (seaweed) strips for wrapping

Instructions:

1. Start by preparing the fish. Remove any skin and bones from the fillets and cut them into small pieces.
2. Place the fish pieces in a food processor and pulse until they form a smooth paste. You can also achieve this by finely chopping the fish with a knife.
3. Transfer the fish paste to a mixing bowl and add the potato starch or cornstarch, salt, sugar, mirin, and soy sauce. Mix everything together until well combined and the mixture becomes smooth.
4. Wet your hands with water to prevent sticking, then shape the fish mixture into long cylindrical shapes, about 4-5 inches in length and 1 inch in diameter. You can shape them by hand or use a bamboo skewer to help mold them.
5. If you're grilling the chikuwa, thread them onto bamboo skewers that have been soaked in water for about 30 minutes. This prevents them from burning on the grill.
6. To cook the chikuwa, you have two options: grilling or frying. If grilling, preheat your grill to medium heat and grill the chikuwa for 4-5 minutes on each side, or until they are cooked through and lightly browned. If frying, heat some oil in a skillet over medium heat and fry the chikuwa for about 3-4 minutes on each side, or until golden brown and cooked through.
7. Once cooked, remove the chikuwa from the grill or skillet and let them cool slightly before serving. If desired, you can wrap each chikuwa with a strip of nori for extra flavor and presentation.

8. Serve the chikuwa fish cakes hot as a snack, appetizer, or part of a larger meal. Enjoy their savory flavor and unique texture!

Kombu dashi broth

Ingredients:

- 20g kombu (dried kelp)
- 4 cups water

Instructions:

1. Start by wiping the surface of the kombu with a damp cloth to remove any dirt or debris. Avoid rinsing it under water as this can wash away some of its flavor.
2. In a large saucepan or pot, add the water and kombu. Allow the kombu to soak in the water for at least 30 minutes to an hour. This helps to extract its flavor.
3. After soaking, place the saucepan over medium heat. Slowly bring the water to just below a simmer; do not let it boil as this can make the kombu release a bitter flavor.
4. Once the water is heated, remove the kombu from the pot using tongs or a slotted spoon. Discard the kombu or save it for another use, such as in a salad or to make furikake seasoning.
5. Your kombu dashi broth is now ready to use! It can be used as a base for soups (like miso soup), sauces, marinades, and more. It adds depth of flavor and umami to a wide range of dishes.
6. Store any leftover kombu dashi in an airtight container in the refrigerator for up to 3-4 days. You can also freeze it in ice cube trays for longer storage.

Enjoy the rich, savory flavor of homemade kombu dashi in your favorite Japanese dishes!

Saba mackerel sushi

Ingredients:

- 2 fresh mackerel fillets, deboned
- 2 cups sushi rice (short-grain Japanese rice)
- 4 tablespoons rice vinegar
- 2 tablespoons sugar
- 1 teaspoon salt
- Nori sheets (seaweed), cut into thin strips (optional, for wrapping)
- Wasabi paste (optional, for serving)
- Pickled ginger (gari) (optional, for serving)
- Soy sauce (shoyu) (optional, for serving)

Instructions:

1. Start by preparing the sushi rice. Rinse the rice under cold water until the water runs clear. Drain the rice and cook it according to the package instructions or using a rice cooker.
2. While the rice is cooking, prepare the seasoning for the rice. In a small saucepan, combine the rice vinegar, sugar, and salt. Heat the mixture over low heat, stirring occasionally, until the sugar and salt are fully dissolved. Remove from heat and let it cool.
3. Once the rice is cooked, transfer it to a large mixing bowl. Gradually pour the seasoned vinegar over the rice while gently folding it in with a spatula or rice paddle. Be careful not to smash the rice grains. Continue folding until the rice is evenly coated with the vinegar mixture.
4. Let the seasoned rice cool to room temperature. While the rice is cooling, prepare the mackerel fillets. Rinse the mackerel under cold water and pat them dry with paper towels. Cut each fillet into thin slices, about 1/4 inch thick.
5. Once the rice has cooled, it's time to assemble the sushi. Take a small handful of seasoned rice and shape it into an oval-shaped mound using your hands.
6. Place a slice of mackerel on top of the rice mound. If desired, you can wrap a strip of nori around the sushi to hold it together.
7. Repeat the process with the remaining rice and mackerel slices until you have made all the sushi.

8. Serve the saba mackerel sushi with wasabi paste, pickled ginger, and soy sauce on the side for dipping, if desired.

Enjoy the delicious flavors of homemade saba mackerel sushi as a delightful appetizer or part of a Japanese-inspired meal!

Kaisendon seafood rice bowl

Ingredients:

For the sushi rice:

- 2 cups sushi rice (short-grain Japanese rice)
- 2 cups water
- 4 tablespoons rice vinegar
- 2 tablespoons sugar
- 1 teaspoon salt

For the toppings:

- Assorted seafood such as tuna, salmon, squid, shrimp, scallops, crab, or any other seafood of your choice, thinly sliced or diced
- Nori sheets (seaweed), cut into thin strips
- Avocado, sliced (optional)
- Cucumber, julienned (optional)
- Radish sprouts (kaiware), for garnish (optional)
- Tobiko (flying fish roe), for garnish (optional)
- Sesame seeds, for garnish (optional)

For the sauce:

- 1/4 cup soy sauce
- 1 tablespoon mirin (Japanese sweet rice wine)
- 1 teaspoon sesame oil
- 1 teaspoon grated ginger
- 1 teaspoon wasabi paste (optional)

Instructions:

1. Start by preparing the sushi rice. Rinse the rice under cold water until the water runs clear. Drain the rice and cook it according to the package instructions or using a rice cooker.
2. While the rice is cooking, prepare the seasoning for the rice. In a small saucepan, combine the rice vinegar, sugar, and salt. Heat the mixture over low heat, stirring occasionally, until the sugar and salt are fully dissolved. Remove from heat and let it cool.
3. Once the rice is cooked, transfer it to a large mixing bowl. Gradually pour the seasoned vinegar over the rice while gently folding it in with a spatula or rice paddle. Be careful not to smash the rice grains. Continue folding until the rice is evenly coated with the vinegar mixture.
4. Let the seasoned rice cool to room temperature.
5. While the rice is cooling, prepare the toppings. Slice or dice the assorted seafood into bite-sized pieces. You can also prepare any optional toppings such as avocado, cucumber, or radish sprouts.
6. In a small bowl, whisk together the ingredients for the sauce: soy sauce, mirin, sesame oil, grated ginger, and wasabi paste (if using).
7. To assemble the kaisendon bowls, divide the sushi rice evenly among serving bowls.
8. Arrange the assorted seafood and any optional toppings on top of the rice in an attractive manner.
9. Drizzle the sauce over the seafood and rice bowls.
10. Garnish with nori strips, tobiko, sesame seeds, and radish sprouts, if desired.
11. Serve the kaisendon bowls immediately and enjoy the vibrant flavors of fresh seafood and sushi rice!

Feel free to customize your kaisendon with your favorite seafood and toppings to create a unique and delicious dish that suits your taste preferences.

Ankake yakisoba noodles with thick sauce

Ingredients:

For the yakisoba noodles:

- 2 packs of yakisoba noodles (or 12 oz of fresh or dried noodles)
- 1 tablespoon oil for frying

For the thick sauce (ankake):

- 2 tablespoons soy sauce
- 2 tablespoons oyster sauce
- 2 tablespoons mirin (Japanese sweet rice wine)
- 1 tablespoon sugar
- 1 tablespoon cornstarch
- 1 cup water

For the stir-fry:

- 1 tablespoon oil for stir-frying
- 1 onion, sliced
- 1 carrot, julienned
- 1 bell pepper, sliced
- 1 cup cabbage, shredded
- 1 cup mushrooms, sliced
- 1 cup protein of your choice (sliced chicken, pork, shrimp, or tofu)
- Optional toppings: sliced green onions, toasted sesame seeds, pickled ginger

Instructions:

1. If using packaged yakisoba noodles, follow the package instructions to prepare them. If using fresh or dried noodles, cook them according to the package instructions, then rinse under cold water and drain well.

2. In a small bowl, mix together the soy sauce, oyster sauce, mirin, sugar, cornstarch, and water to make the thick sauce (ankake). Set aside.
3. Heat 1 tablespoon of oil in a large skillet or wok over medium-high heat. Add the sliced onion, carrot, bell pepper, cabbage, mushrooms, and protein of your choice to the skillet. Stir-fry for 3-4 minutes, or until the vegetables are tender and the protein is cooked through.
4. Push the stir-fried vegetables and protein to one side of the skillet, and add another tablespoon of oil to the empty side. Add the cooked yakisoba noodles to the skillet and stir-fry for 2-3 minutes, breaking up any clumps with a spatula.
5. Pour the thick sauce (ankake) over the noodles and vegetables in the skillet. Stir well to coat everything evenly in the sauce.
6. Continue to cook for another 2-3 minutes, or until the sauce has thickened and everything is heated through.
7. Remove the skillet from the heat and transfer the Ankake Yakisoba noodles to serving plates.
8. Garnish with sliced green onions, toasted sesame seeds, and pickled ginger, if desired.
9. Serve the Ankake Yakisoba noodles hot and enjoy their savory flavor and satisfying texture!

Feel free to customize this dish by adding your favorite vegetables or protein, and adjust the thickness of the sauce according to your preference.

Kinpira gobo sautéed burdock root

Ingredients:

- 2 medium-sized burdock roots (gobo)
- 1 carrot
- 2 tablespoons vegetable oil
- 2 tablespoons soy sauce
- 2 tablespoons mirin (Japanese sweet rice wine)
- 1 tablespoon sugar
- 1 tablespoon sesame oil
- Toasted sesame seeds (for garnish, optional)

Instructions:

1. Start by preparing the burdock roots (gobo). Peel the outer skin of the burdock roots using a vegetable peeler or a knife. Then, cut the peeled burdock roots into thin matchsticks or julienne strips.
2. Peel the carrot and cut it into thin matchsticks or julienne strips similar in size to the burdock root.
3. Place the burdock root and carrot strips in a bowl of cold water and let them soak for about 5-10 minutes. This helps to remove any bitterness from the burdock root and prevents it from turning brown.
4. Heat the vegetable oil in a large skillet or wok over medium heat. Add the drained burdock root and carrot strips to the skillet and sauté for 2-3 minutes, stirring constantly.
5. In a small bowl, mix together the soy sauce, mirin, sugar, and sesame oil to make the sauce.
6. Pour the sauce over the burdock root and carrot mixture in the skillet. Continue to sauté for another 5-7 minutes, or until the vegetables are tender and the sauce has thickened slightly.
7. Once the vegetables are cooked through and the sauce has thickened, remove the skillet from the heat.
8. Transfer the Kinpira Gobo to a serving dish and garnish with toasted sesame seeds, if desired.
9. Serve the Kinpira Gobo hot or at room temperature as a delicious side dish or topping for rice.

Enjoy the savory-sweet flavor and crunchy texture of homemade Kinpira Gobo!

Natto fermented soybeans

Ingredients:

- 2 cups soybeans
- Natto starter culture (can be purchased online or from specialty stores)
- Water

Equipment:

- Pressure cooker or large pot
- Glass or plastic container with a lid
- Cheesecloth or clean kitchen towel
- Oven with a light bulb or a yogurt maker (optional)

Instructions:

1. Rinse the soybeans under cold water and remove any debris or impurities.
2. Soak the soybeans in water overnight or for at least 8 hours. The beans will absorb water and expand, making them easier to cook.
3. Drain the soaked soybeans and transfer them to a pressure cooker or large pot. Add enough water to cover the beans by about 2 inches.
4. Cook the soybeans according to the instructions for your pressure cooker or simmer them on the stovetop until they are soft and cooked through. This usually takes about 1-2 hours.
5. Once the soybeans are cooked, drain them and let them cool to room temperature.
6. Transfer the cooked soybeans to a clean glass or plastic container with a lid. Sprinkle the natto starter culture over the soybeans and gently mix them together.
7. Cover the container with a piece of cheesecloth or a clean kitchen towel and secure it with the lid. This allows air to circulate while preventing dust or insects from getting into the beans.
8. Place the container in a warm, dark place with a temperature of around 100-110°F (37-43°C). You can use an oven with a light bulb on or a yogurt maker to maintain the temperature, or simply wrap the container in a warm blanket.

9. Let the soybeans ferment for about 24-48 hours, depending on your preference for flavor and texture. During this time, the beans will develop their characteristic sticky texture and strong aroma.
10. Once the natto is ready, transfer it to the refrigerator to stop the fermentation process and chill it before serving.
11. Serve the natto as a topping for rice, mixed with soy sauce and mustard, or in sushi rolls. Enjoy the unique flavor and health benefits of homemade natto!

Note: Natto has a strong flavor and aroma that may not be to everyone's taste. If you're new to natto, you may want to start with a small amount and gradually increase your intake as you acquire a taste for it.

Horenso no gomaae spinach salad with sesame dressing

Ingredients:

- 1 bunch spinach
- 2 tablespoons sesame seeds
- 1 tablespoon soy sauce
- 1 tablespoon sugar
- 1 tablespoon mirin (Japanese sweet rice wine)
- 1 tablespoon sesame oil

Instructions:

1. Wash the spinach thoroughly under cold water to remove any dirt or debris. Trim off any tough stems or wilted leaves.
2. Bring a pot of water to a boil and blanch the spinach for about 1-2 minutes, or until it wilts but still retains some texture. Immediately transfer the blanched spinach to a bowl of ice water to stop the cooking process and preserve its vibrant green color.
3. Drain the cooled spinach and squeeze out any excess water. Then, gently squeeze small bundles of spinach to form oblong shapes.
4. Toast the sesame seeds in a dry skillet over medium heat until they become fragrant and golden brown, about 2-3 minutes. Be careful not to burn them.
5. Grind the toasted sesame seeds in a suribachi (Japanese mortar and pestle) or a spice grinder until they form a coarse paste.
6. In a small bowl, mix together the ground sesame seeds, soy sauce, sugar, mirin, and sesame oil to make the dressing.
7. Arrange the squeezed spinach on a serving plate or individual plates.
8. Drizzle the sesame dressing over the spinach just before serving. You can also sprinkle additional toasted sesame seeds on top for extra flavor and texture.
9. Serve the Horenso no Gomaae spinach salad as a side dish or appetizer. Enjoy the delicious combination of tender spinach and nutty sesame dressing!

This salad is simple yet packed with flavor, making it a perfect addition to any Japanese meal.

Saba shioyaki grilled salted mackerel

Ingredients:

- 2 fresh mackerel fillets, cleaned and gutted
- Coarse sea salt
- Lemon wedges (for serving, optional)

Instructions:

1. Preheat your grill or broiler to medium-high heat. If using a broiler, position the rack about 6 inches away from the heat source.
2. Pat the mackerel fillets dry with paper towels to remove any excess moisture.
3. Score the skin of each mackerel fillet with diagonal cuts, about 1/4 inch deep, at 1-inch intervals. This helps the fish cook evenly and allows the salt to penetrate the flesh.
4. Generously sprinkle both sides of each mackerel fillet with coarse sea salt, rubbing it into the flesh and skin.
5. Place the salted mackerel fillets on the preheated grill or under the broiler, skin-side down. Grill or broil for 4-5 minutes on each side, or until the skin is crispy and the flesh is opaque and flakes easily with a fork.
6. Carefully flip the mackerel fillets halfway through the cooking time to ensure even cooking.
7. Once the mackerel is cooked through and golden brown on both sides, remove it from the grill or broiler.
8. Transfer the grilled salted mackerel fillets to a serving platter and garnish with lemon wedges, if desired.
9. Serve the Saba Shioyaki immediately while hot, accompanied by steamed rice and your favorite vegetables.

Enjoy the delicious simplicity of Saba Shioyaki, savoring the natural flavors of the mackerel enhanced by the seasoning of salt and a hint of smokiness from the grill!

Kurimu korokke creamy croquettes

Ingredients:

For the filling:

- 2 medium potatoes, peeled and diced
- 1 small onion, finely chopped
- 1/2 cup ground meat (pork, beef, or chicken)
- 2 tablespoons butter
- 2 tablespoons all-purpose flour
- 1 cup milk
- Salt and pepper to taste
- Pinch of nutmeg (optional)
- Chopped parsley or green onions for garnish (optional)

For the breading:

- All-purpose flour for dredging
- 2 large eggs, beaten
- Panko breadcrumbs for coating
- Vegetable oil for frying

Instructions:

1. Start by making the creamy filling. Place the diced potatoes in a pot of salted water and boil until tender, about 10-15 minutes. Drain well and mash the cooked potatoes with a potato masher or fork until smooth. Set aside.
2. In a separate skillet, heat 1 tablespoon of butter over medium heat. Add the chopped onion and ground meat, and cook until the meat is browned and the onion is soft and translucent. Season with salt, pepper, and nutmeg, if using.
3. Add the remaining 1 tablespoon of butter to the skillet and sprinkle the flour over the meat mixture. Cook, stirring constantly, for 1-2 minutes to cook off the raw flour taste.

4. Gradually pour in the milk, stirring continuously to prevent lumps from forming. Cook the mixture until it thickens and resembles a creamy sauce.
5. Combine the mashed potatoes with the creamy meat mixture, stirring until well combined. Adjust the seasoning if necessary. Remove from heat and let the filling cool slightly.
6. Once the filling has cooled, shape it into small patties or cylinders, about 2 inches in diameter and 1 inch thick. Place the patties on a baking sheet lined with parchment paper and chill in the refrigerator for at least 30 minutes to firm up.
7. Prepare three shallow bowls for breading: one with all-purpose flour, one with beaten eggs, and one with panko breadcrumbs.
8. Dredge each chilled croquette in flour, shaking off any excess. Dip it into the beaten eggs, then coat it evenly with panko breadcrumbs, pressing gently to adhere.
9. Heat vegetable oil in a deep skillet or frying pan to 350°F (180°C). Carefully add the breaded croquettes to the hot oil in batches, taking care not to overcrowd the pan.
10. Fry the croquettes until they are golden brown and crispy on all sides, about 3-4 minutes per side.
11. Once cooked, transfer the Kurimu Korokke to a plate lined with paper towels to drain off any excess oil.
12. Serve the creamy croquettes hot, garnished with chopped parsley or green onions if desired. Enjoy their crispy exterior and creamy, flavorful filling!

Kurimu Korokke makes a delicious appetizer, side dish, or main course when served with a side salad or steamed vegetables.

Matcha latte

Ingredients:

- 1 teaspoon matcha powder
- 2 tablespoons hot water
- 1 cup milk (dairy or plant-based)
- Sweetener of your choice (optional), such as sugar, honey, or maple syrup

Instructions:

1. Heat the milk: Pour the milk into a small saucepan and heat it over medium-low heat until it's warm but not boiling. You can also heat the milk in the microwave if you prefer.
2. Prepare the matcha: In a small bowl, sift the matcha powder to remove any lumps. Add the hot water and whisk vigorously until the matcha is fully dissolved and a smooth paste forms.
3. Froth the milk (optional): If you have a milk frother, you can use it to froth the warm milk until it becomes foamy. Alternatively, you can skip this step if you prefer your latte without froth.
4. Combine the matcha and milk: Pour the matcha paste into a mug. Slowly pour the warm frothed milk over the matcha paste, using a spoon to hold back the foam if desired. Stir well to combine the matcha and milk.
5. Sweeten to taste: If you like your latte sweetened, add your preferred sweetener to taste and stir until it's fully dissolved.
6. Enjoy: Your Matcha Latte is now ready to enjoy! Serve it hot and savor the delicious combination of creamy milk and earthy matcha flavor.

Feel free to adjust the ratio of matcha to milk and the sweetness level according to your taste preferences. You can also customize your latte by adding a sprinkle of cinnamon or a dash of vanilla extract for extra flavor. Enjoy!